AMAZON FBA

2019

BLAKE DAVIS

TABLE OF CONTENTS

INTRODUCTION

A question that is on many people's mind is "What Is Amazon FBA"? To help me explain what Amazon FBA is, let us look at a little tale, of how Amazon FBA can help you take your online trading business to the next level.

Amazon FBA or to give it full name Fulfilment By Amazon is a program set up by Amazon that allows you to use Amazon to warehouse and then send out your purchases (but always let you sell your items on the Amazon Site). Amazon FBA is very straightforward, but at the same time very persuasive and can take your trades to the next level for very low costs.

Imagine the scene: you are working on your product sourcing and have chosen some books, CD's DVD's, home and Beauty items and few new toys (items sold via Amazon FBA have to be either new or collectible). Now normally at the back of your mind you have a thought "I wish I could buy more stock" but there is no more room in your home; This is where the Amazon FBA comes into play. You can just test the water out by using the basic Amazon selling account or you can be a Pro-Merchant, it doesn't matter.

First: You go home and scan or list the items as usual into your Amazon selling account and a few clicks later, you print out some bar codes which you must put over the original bar code on the item (Items will need to have a bar code or listed on the Amazon site). A few more clicks and you print out a packing slip which goes in the box or boxes. You then book a pick-up from a carrier (this does depend on where you live and how you pay for it - each country is different)

Second: you complete the order and wait for the order to be picked up and within days your item will be in the Amazon warehouse being sold for you then you can sit back and bank the money. Amazon FBA deals with payments, shipping and customer emails, you just need to source more stock and bank the money.

Yes there are some extra costs that Amazon charges but these are low, and the savings you make on the postage is fantastic - remember you are using Amazon's buying power and no more queues in Post Offices and no more having to buy bubble wrap and boxes.

Something else people do not realize is that you can use Amazon FBA to ship out to your eBay and other buyers. Amazon store the items and send the items out for you, for a very little cost and in most cases a lot cheaper than you can think. All the pricing information can be found on your countries Amazon site, just do a search for Amazon FBA.

Go on and give it a go, you have nothing to lose and a lot to gain.

WHAT IS THE AMAZON FBA PROGRAM ALL ABOUT?

FBA is a service Amazon arrange to allow online and offline sellers to send their goods to Amazon. Amazon will pack and send the products to individual customers on your behalf. You may not know how big the Amazon marketplace is, if you don't use regularly. They have grown from just selling books to now selling just about anything.

You may also sell products on Amazon and do not use their FBA service, shipping your own products. As you see there are many advantages of using the FBA system which will give you more free time and provide a more automated business solution.

There are similar services that other drop shippers provide but Amazon hold your own goods in one of their fulfillment centres. The service will send your goods anytime and anywhere on your behalf. This system can be further integrated with your website to create a virtually fully automated system to send your goods through Amazon and for Amazon shipping them to customers. The costs for the service are very competitive and you only pay for actual storage and shipments at discount Amazon's rates as they don't charge a fee to use the system.

So why should you consider using Amazon's system?

Here are some of the key points to the FBA system:

-You can sell almost anything on Amazon or through your own website and have them pack and sent.

-By automating your website with Amazon, the business can run on autopilot and you can take time away if you choose and your business still functions.

-Send all your stock to Amazon and they will handle everything all you have to do is collect your profits.

-Amazon is now outranking eBay on Alexa for traffic they are indeed a major competitor to eBay.

-Some eBay sellers are using the Amazon FBA to ship goods sold through eBay.

CHAPTER 1

WHAT IS AMAZON FBA?

As a business maker or individual who is looking to trade products on Amazon, having the opportunity to take FBA can be quite beneficial. With the ability to cut off the amount of time that you would spend selling and shipping your products, Fulfillment by Amazon does most of the business for you. If you're presently interested in these services, below is information and how it can be useful for your selling needs.

The Fulfillment Procedure

The entire process is relatively easy. You will be provided with the opportunity to store your items in one of Amazon's fulfillment centers. Once a client purchases something that you have for sale, they will surely pick, pack, and ship it for you. Also, customer service will be provided to each product that you are wanting to sell. That means that if your buyer has any questions, customer service will answer and help.

Fees

Another large benefit associated with using Amazon FBA is that you will be able to take advantage of their services for a minimal fee. As a more cost-effective solution than opening your own warehouse and packing/shipping your own goods, you can eliminate this time-consuming task without having to pay outrageous fees. You will be able to pay as you go when you start working with Amazon. Each company will be charged by the space that you use in the warehouse and the amount of orders that Amazon fulfills.

What to Sell Using Amazon FBA

One of the biggest advantages associated with using Amazon's Fulfillment to sell your goods is that there are dozens of different categories that let you know what to sell. The majority of sellers list their products in the "Open Categories" section due to the fact that listing products under these categories does not require approval. Some of the open categories available to companies include:

- Kindle by Amazon
- Any Book
- Baby and children items
- Photos and cameras
- Cellphones
- Garden and home items
- Electronics

The other lists available for people looking to sell using Amazon FBA are known as "Professional sellers Categories". In order to list your products here, you will need approval. Some of these categories include:

- Powersports and Automotive
- Beauty products
- Memorabilia Coins
- Clothing and accessories
- Beaux arts
- Bonus cards
- Food and grocery

HOW AMAZON FBA HELPS ENTREPRENEURS

Amazon FBA is an amazing way to ensure you have products sold and shipped directly to customers therefore you don't have to worry about the shipping and handling procedure. It can also be quite useful for businesses who are unable to have a enough amount of storage space for their goods, as they house your products on-site. With that being said, Fulfillment By Amazon is essentially the perfect component for every seller. Prior to signing up, it is advised that you ensure that it is the right offer for you by determining how your products reach your customers, how you can have control of the process and the scalability of the program.

How Your Products Reach Amazon Prime Customers

The number one component to consider when selling with Fulfillment By Amazon is how your products will reach Amazon Prime customers. When you use Amazon FBA, all of your customers that have an Amazon Prime account will be provided with the opportunity to select two-day shipping for free. Alongside Prime customers, regular Amazon customers will be able to take advantage of the free shipping with orders of $35.00 or more. One of the largest benefits associated with listing with FBA is that your products will be listed without a shipping cost for Amazon Prime customers, allowing you to increase your sales.

What is Amazon FBA Seller Central?

Amazon FBA Seller Central is the aspect of the Amazon website that you will be able to use to have full control over what warehouse your items will be stocked in, how you want to list your items, and how you will display the selling features of your products. It is essentially an entire dashboard dedicated to your products and how they will be seen by the public. You will be able to search for your products once they have been added, look at the other prices of competing FBA sellers, and determine what steps you want Amazon to take during the sale such as shipping the products. Seller Central is imperative to the selling process as it will provide the "first impression" that your customers receive when they find your products.

What is the Scalability of Amazon FBA?

Amazon FBA scalability is another important factor to consider when working with Amazon. As your business grows, you will want to ensure that Amazon will grow with you to make sure that each order is fulfilled efficiently. With scalability offered by the program, you can rest assured that Amazon will be able to assist you during peak seasons and offer more resources when you are selling more products. With the ability to pack and ship either a single unit or thousands of different units, the options are endless.

CHAPTER 2

14 RULES BEHIND AMAZON'S FIERCE WORKPLACE

Many of Amazon's competitive tricks are guided by what the company calls its "Leadership Principles".

The 14 rules are a summary for how employees are expected to think through new ideas and constantly improve their trades.

Customer addiction: Leaders start with the clients and work backwards. They work strenuously, to earn and keep customer trust. Although leaders pay attention to contestants they're addicted over customers.

Ownership: Leaders are holders. They think long term and don't sacrifice long-term value for short-term results. They act on behalf of the whole company, after just their own team. They never think or say "that's not my job."

Invent and make more intelligible: Leaders await and require transformation and invention from their teams and always find ways to simplify. They are outwardly aware, look for new ideas from anywhere, and are not limited by "not invented here." As we make new things, we accept that we may be mistaken for a long period of time.

Leaders are right quite a lot: They are indeed. They have stable business judgment and instincts. They search different perspectives and work to disprove their beliefs.

Appoint and develop the Best: Leaders promotes the performance bar with every hire and promotion. They perceive exceptional talent and willingly move them all through the organization. Leader's develop leaders and take seriously their part in coaching others. We labor on behalf of our people to design mechanisms for development like Career Choice.

Reiterate on the Highest Standards: Leaders have relentlessly high standards — lots of people may think these standards are inappropriately high. Leaders are continually raising the bar and driving their teams to provide high quality products, services, and processes. Leaders ensure that faulty products do not get sent down the line and that problems are fixed so they stay fixed.

Think Big: Thinking small is a self-fulfilling prophecy. Leaders create and communicate a bold direction that inspires results. They think differently and look around corners for ways to serve customers.

Bias for Action: Speed matters in business. Many decisions and actions are reversible and do not need extensive study. We should value calculated risk taking.

Frugality: Accomplish more with less. Constraints breed resourcefulness, self-sufficiency and invention. There are no extra points for growing headcount, budget size, or fixed expense.

Learn and Be Curious: Leaders are never done learning and always seek to improve themselves. They are curious about new possibilities and act to explore them.

Earn Trust: Leaders listen attentively, speak candidly, and treat others respectfully. They are vocally self-critical, even when doing so is awkward or embarrassing. Leaders do not believe their or their team's body odor smells of perfume. They benchmark themselves and their teams against the best.

Dive Deep: Leaders operate at all levels, stay connected to the details, audit frequently, and are skeptical when metrics and anecdote differ. No task is beneath them.

Have Backbone; Disagree and Commit: Leaders are obligated to respectfully challenge decisions when they disagree, even when doing so is uncomfortable or exhausting. Leaders have conviction and are tenacious. They do not compromise for the sake of social cohesion. Once a decision is determined, they commit wholly.

Provide results: Leaders focus on the key inputs for their business and provide the right quality and in a timely fashion. Despite delays, they rise to the occasion and never relax.

FBA GLOBAL SELLING

We're all aware of how difficult international business can be. Apart from fulfilling your orders, careful thoughts such as import taxes, customs duties, currency conversion, regional laws or rules, language barriers and local cultures can all add more difficulties for selling your products in international markets. For small businesses with capital restrictions and lower risk tolerance, Amazon's Global Selling, joint with FBA services, allow them to enter a new market and test out products with little investment and risk. Before you make the choice to enter a target market, you must conduct some market research to make sure your product is sellable in the region.

Amazon Global Selling is intercede to help companies find the information they need to sell to the right markets.

"Sellable" generally means your product is in concession with the target country's regulations and specifications, but that's not enough. Say you're a North American corporation of electronic devices, and you decide to sell your items in Japan. You re-work your actual products to meet Japan's electrical specifications, only to discover there is no request for that product in the region.

CHAPTER 3

BENEFIT OF USING FULFILMENT BY AMAZON

How does FBA look like and how does it work? Can you redeem money or enjoy other benefits with this offer or procedure?

FBA is a process through which Amazon keeps a stock of a seller's items and then list them on their site for sale. Apart from this, the company receives payments for each order placed online and the delivers the specific goods to each client.

Along with this process, a lot of stores have enjoyed a good deal of growth in their sales. Some stores have Amazon complete the orders for their items. Typically, the goods are sent directly to the buyers by the sellers that sells directly on Amazon. Sometimes it happens by the sellers on other websites, such as Etsy, eBay that move to the FBA. So, it's interesting to know how this offer by the big store has helped people all over the world.

According to many sellers, they have experienced a significant rise in their sales volume. On the other hand, buyers believe that they are purchasing from a trustworthy company instead of an individual. In other words, buying directly via FBA adds to the trust of the buyer in the supplier therefore they may buy again down the road.

Aside from this, sellers can make use of this offer in order to achieve many other benefits. If you use this service as a seller, you won't have to worry about the promotion of the product. Moreover, it will be Amazon's responsibility to deal with buyers and fulfill orders. On the other hand, you can focus on other tasks, such as getting new products and do other tasks that may make your business even bigger.

Additional benefits:

If you are a product owner, you can take some days off without worrying about who will take care of your business while you are away. Your business will keep running while you are having a great time with your friends in Paris. So, you can stay away from your office for as many days as you want. As long as Amazon has your products in their stock, you are good to go and you don't need to worry about anything.

Some people just don't like to deal with buyers directly. They find it hard to deal with difficult customers. Dealing with stress is not their cup of tea. All of these things will be handled by Amazon.

3 Reasons to Use Fulfillment by Amazon

1. Buyers will know that your products are in stock. When a buyer sees an FBA listing, they know the product is in stock and it will be shipped directly from Amazon's warehouse. Non-FBA sellers may cancel an order for different reasons, but with FBA, the buyer can be assured that this will not happen. This is particularly important during the holiday season when buyers count on receiving their order on time. There is nothing worse than a buyer who is disappointed because they did not receive their item in time for the holidays. By using Amazon fulfillment, buyers know that the product will be professionally packed and will arrive in a timely manner.

2. FBA products are eligible for Amazon Prime. Prime is a service which allows unlimited free two-day shipping on all Amazon purchases and costs $79 dollars per year. In addition to Amazon's own items, FBA items from third party sellers are eligible for Prime as well. This means that your business has access to some of Amazon's best clients. Prime customer's purchase a lot of items, particularly during the holiday season. Prime customers enjoy the free shipping! When you use FBA, you have actually an advantage over other sellers who do not use it, since a buyer who has the Prime service will usually choose your

item over you non-FBA competition. They can get your product with free two-day shipping, which they cannot have from you non-FBA competition.

3. You will spend less time on customer service. FBA takes care all customer service for you buyers. This means that if your buyer has any issue with their order, they can get in touch with Amazon Customer Service directly. You will save an enormous amount of time and afflictions when you do not need to manage your own customer service.

If you are a third-party seller on Amazon, using FBA will give you more time to spend on the most important aspect of your business: finding new inventory. With more time to find good inventory, your business profit should greatly increase.

CREATE YOUR OWN AMAZON SELLER ACCOUNT

You've done all the thinking, market research, and ordering of your new items. You've even got a smooth business plan. Since you've decided that opening a Fulfillment by Amazon's (FBA) business is right for you, now you're probably asking yourself how to set up your store so you can start selling your products.

It might seem a little intimidating to set up your Amazon Seller account, especially if this is your first online retail business. Luckily, it's really simple, and as long as you've got all the pieces in place, you'll be selling in no time.

It's important to take the time to prepare your store for customers, but once your account is all set up, you can add your inventory and get your store up and running!

Before diving into the step-by-step process of setting up your Amazon Seller account and your Seller Central space, there are a few things you need to have completed ahead of time to make sure the setup process goes as smoothly as possible:

Figuring out what you're selling and how you're sourcing your product are the most time-consuming parts of setting up your FBA business. Make sure you've already done these tasks before you go through the effort of setting up your account so you can start selling right away. If you haven't done this step yet, make sure you do your research on what products will help you excel as an Amazon Seller.

Besides knowing what product you're selling; you should probably decide on the name of your store before you create your account. Are you going to use your individual name, or do you have a business or brand name already decided on?

Most importantly, you need to know if you're going to be creating the account as a business or as an individual. Amazon has two different account options for sellers depending on their situation, but you'll also need to have this decision made ahead of time for tax purposes, since you'll need to fill out tax forms while setting up your account.

Once you have these things squared away, you'll have all the key background information that will help you set up your store in a super-streamlined fashion.

Your Choice: Professional or Individual?

It might sound like a no-brainer question ("Of course I'm a professional!"), but these are Amazon's choices for your seller account plan. It's worth exploring your options before you start the process of creating your account, since there are pretty big differences between the two.

Either way, you'll be able to sell your items and run your FBA business; the major difference has to do with whether you think you'll be selling more or less than 40 items per month (and whether you want to pay a monthly fee).

The Individual seller plan doesn't have a monthly fee, and this plan is pretty appealing if you're just starting out and in a more experimental mode with your products.

If you're feeling pretty confident that your item's going to sell like hotcakes, however, it might be worth it to pay $39.99 per month to be a Professional seller. That way, you won't have to pay Amazon $0.99 for each item sold, which is the fee that Individual sellers have to pay.

If you want to wait and see how your FBA does, you can start as an Individual and upgrade your account to the Professional selling plan at any time. There's a lot of overlap between the two plans: Both Individuals and Professionals have to pay shipping, referral, and closing fees, all explained on Amazon's website. And both Professional and Individual sellers can list their products in more than 20 categories, but Professional sellers can include their products in 10 extra categories.

Form Your Amazon Seller Account

Before starting your Amazon's website in the thrilling rush to open your new FBA business, make sure you have these important items right next to you:

1) A credit card that can be re – charged internationally.

2) Your banking data, such as your routing and account numbers.

3) Your tax ID either for yourself or your business.

CHAPTER 4

PRODUCT RESEARCH TOOLS IN AMAZON

In surveys, Amazon FBA sellers say that items research is the most time-consuming – and most discouraging – aspect of the selling process. These days there are a number of dissimilar research tools available to sellers.

1. Jungle scout

The very popular Jungle Scout is a firm favorite among Amazon sellers.

Available as a web app or Chrome extension, Jungle Scout it's well known to take the guesswork out of product research in order to minimize the risks and maximize the possible profit.

The web app allows users to search through thousands of products, pinpoints the most profitable and keep an eye on the competition.

2. AMZ Scout

AMZ Scout is known as one of the most reliable and accurate product research tools on the market, and it's a great Jungle Scout alternative.

With a tagline of 'The Smart Choice for Making Smart Decisions,' Amz Scout is a comprehensive and competitive way of finding products and keeping track of sales.

3. Unicorn Smasher

Everybody loves a unicorn and, the Unicorn Smasher product research tool earns its place on the leaderboard of the best available.

Features include comprehensive data and accurate sales estimates and allows users to move quickly and easily between product niches.

4. AMZ Base

Amz Base is a great tool to help sellers to quickly search and identify the right products to sell on Amazon and, one of the best things about it is that it's free!

Sellers can quickly and easily use the tool to find descriptions and ASIN numbers of products on Amazon as well as calculating FBA fees.

5. Amazon Best Sellers

Amazon Best sellers is an extremely useful way of quickly getting an idea of the kind of products which sell well on Amazon. Categorized by product genre for easy filtering and searching, the page is great for those who do not yet know what they want to sell on Amazon. Clearly laid out and easy to understand, the Amazon Best seller's page allows users to make an informed choice based on price and popularity.

6. Amazon Hot New Releases

Amazon Hot New Releases is a regularly updated catalog of new and trending products on Amazon. Set out in clearly defined categories, the page allows Amazon sellers to browse all products or to navigate straight to a particular product genre such as electronics, children's products, popular books and movies and clothing and accessories.

7. Amazon Movers & Shakers

Perfect for FBA Sellers, the Amazon Movers & Shakers page is updated hourly and is an overview of products with the biggest sales rank gains within the past 24 hours. Listed by category such as books, electronics and toys, the page shows the sales rank and percentage increase for each product, allowing users to see at a glance the products which are performing particularly well.

8. Amazon Most Wished For

The Amazon Most Wished For page is an overview of the products which have been added to Amazon wish lists the most times. This is a really good tool for giving sellers an indication of the products which buyers find interesting.

9. Kickstarter

Kickstarter is a crowdfunding site which allows people to raise money for personal projects and causes such as the development of a new clothing range or a charitable project. Although not specifically a selling site, Amazon sellers can browse through current projects to find out the kind of products that are being developed for sale in order to plan ahead for future sales.

10. Indiegogo

Another crowdfunding site, Indiegogo allows users to raise funds to develop anything from clothing lines to new innovations in electronics. By raising money on the site, the developer is able to buy the materials and services necessary to get their project off the ground.

Not only can Amazon sellers use the site for product ideas but may even want to get involved with a campaign with a view to a future partnership.

11. Watched Item

Watched Item is a quick and easy way of identifying and tracking items on Ebay which have the most interest without having to make hundreds of individual searches.

Ebay's 'watch' option allows potential buyers to bookmark a particular sale and to receive updates on how the auction is progressing in order to be able to wait until the last moment before bidding on that item.

The Watched Item site allows Amazon sellers to search by country or product or by the products with the highest number of current watchers in order to see which products are the most popular.

5 WAYS TO FIND THE BEST PRODUCTS TO SELL ON AMAZON

With the event of the internet in the 90's, Ecommerce has blowout like wildfire. Consumers have passed from traditional shopping to ecommerce.

Today, Amazon has become synonymous with ecommerce. Apart from being a very good online store, it is known for its user personalization attributes. A study by Internet Retailer says that in 2016, Amazon accounted for 43% of all online sales in the US. That alone is a good reason for you to thinking of selling on Amazon.

In fact, people have been known to make as much as $5000 in an hour by selling on Amazon. However, this can be a little tricky. Keep in mind that Amazon sells more than 300 million individual products. And only by selling the right products you can become a successful seller.

Here are five ways to find the best products to sell on Amazon.

1. Start by Discovering Profitable Products

You can find the most profitable items to sell on Amazon without much experience. Amazon provides you all the necessary information to understand market trends and products that sell.

You need to understand what makes an item profitable. Criteria like, shipping weight, popularity, category, and competition all play a major role here. You need to identify products that meet most of the criteria.

Research the Shippable and Sellable Factors

While looking for products you need to first consider three things: Shipping cost, wholesale pricing, and Amazon Seller fees.

Try to buy products considering the following specs:

➢ The price should be 25% to 35% of your target selling price

➢ Your target selling cost should be in the range of $10 to $50

➢ The products should be light in terms of weight i.e., around 2-3 lbs. including box and packaging

➢ Simple and durable items that would reduce the risk of loss from damage

➢ Evergreen or everyday use items, meaning they can be used for the whole the year

➢ Better quality products when compared with competitors.

2. Check For competitors

To bring in returns, you need a product that is rightly priced found and shipped easily, and in demand.

Below are the key factors that determine whether your products meet these criteria.

➢ Products that are not usually being sold by major brands and Amazon sellers

➢ Similar items that have Amazon's Best-Seller Rank (BSR) of 5000 or less.

> ➤ Items that can be searched under different product categories and keywords

> ➤ Leading items keywords having not more than 10,000 searches/month

> ➤ Similar items listings having less than 50 reviews

3. Acquiring knowledge From Amazon Product Listings

Here's an Amazon bestselling game called What Do You Meme. In the product description, you can find all the information on what makes it a seller's goldmine.

In the product description, you will find various information about the product, such as product dimension, weight, etc. From there, you can determine if your product is an evergreen one.

Lookout for the following criteria to find the most sellable and profitable items:

Item pricing: The item is sold at $29.99. The costing is perfect as it falls under the pricing bracket of $10 to $50.

Product measures and weight: There you can find that the product weighs 2.78 pounds and measures of 6.5 x 4.5 x 3 inches. This size and weight will help in reduce the shipping cost.

Overall characteristics and sales ranking: You will see that the Amazon BSR of this product is 3. This is way lower the BSR 5000 rank. Also, it can be found in the toys and games category easily.

Customer analyses: You will find that the item has more than 2000 reviews from consumers. This is way above the 500+ reviews rank making it a well-trusted product. This also indicates that the product has a lot of requests in the market.

4. Find Out What Others are Selling

Do you know that small-scale sellers are making it big by selling niche items? From handmade items to custom and unique jewelry items and even live bugs. In this way, they reduce the competition from large sellers and from Amazon itself.

Amazon is really good when it comes to upselling products. It keeps a section showcasing recommended products underneath a product's description. This encourages buyers to consider the products that are being showcased.

Here's an example:

Notice how Amazon suggests product pairing with the above-mentioned best-seller. Here, suggested products may not be "bestsellers" themselves, but as a seller, you can determine what are the products other sellers are selling.

5. Select Your Source For Products

Once you are done researching on which products to sell, you should start thinking about sourcing them.

Here are two places from where you can start your search:

Alibaba: If you are planning to sell on Amazon, Alibaba is a good place to source your products. It is a place where you can source inexpensive imports. A good thing about Alibaba is that it helps you learn about product sourcing. This is extremely helpful if you are new to the business.

Wholesale marketplaces: Wholesale buyers markets are another way of sourcing your products. Wholesale markets are situated in every major city in the US. And the best part is, they focus on every imaginable industry. To locate your nearest wholesale market just google it. Also, don't forget to add the product name or category you are interested in.

CHAPTER 5

A FIVE-STEP GUIDE TO COMPETE WITH AMAZON

Competing with Amazon is attainable. I'm not saying you can overthrow the ecommerce giant from her throne, but you can surely rank for keywords, sell amazing stuff, and not get absolutely beated by them.

I want to tell you how to do that in actually 5 simple steps.

First, let's talk about what you cannot do. Admitting your errors is the first step to maximizing your strengths.

You cannot have the same size of inventory. Amazon basically owns every consumer product in the world, therefore yeah good luck with that. You're going to need some bigger places to store the stuff.

You cannot have Jeff Bezos. Unless you have a real good offer for him.

You can't have the name amazon.com. It's already been taken, and is not on sale. I have checked for you.

1. Tighten your niche.

Amazon's weakness is in its greatness. It has everything for sale. Amazon can be good at everything.

What about You? You don't sell everything. You just sell a few things. (At least you should.)

You will have a much harder time trying to rank for a lot of different keywords, even if they are all sort of in the same niche. Whatever you sell, Amazon probably has a few more variations, sizes, colors, and features.

2. Do something radical with shipping.

One area that Amazon has completely dominated is the area of shipping. It is, in fact, one of the company's greatest successes.

Members of Amazon's Prime service can get two-day shipping for free, and next-day shipping for just a few dollars on each order. And same-day shipping? Yep, they offer that, too.

3. Create a subscription service.

Another way that Amazon has increased revenue is by creating subscription services:

- Subscribe and save (repeated shipments)
- Amazon Prime (fees paid annually)
- Amazon Simple Storage Service (AWS)

Because they're so good at this repeating payment thing, Amazon actually launched a new service called Amazon Payments with what they can help other companies keep charging customers on a daily basis. You might start seeing more of that quintessential yellow button on the web:

The subscription service is one of the smartest ways to sell a product. You don't just get a one-and-done transactional experience with your customer. Instead, you get a relationship, and revenue every month or year.

You don't have to be a software provider to make the subscription model work. Any form of recurring deliverables warrants recurring payments.

4. Boast the best customer service experience on the planet.

I mean no disrespect to Amazon, but they can't do customer service the way you can. They're too big.

This is a sandbox that Amazon can't play in. But you can.

One of the best ways to compete with Amazon is to provide something that they can't. They can't provide personalized, one-on-one service to human beings like you can.

Your brand can achieve viral spread ability through passionate brand evangelists.

5. Build a fanatical fan base.

Building a jumping, screaming, raving, fanatical fan base is not easy, but it is possible. The strategy is to stay small, at least as it pertains to customer interaction. Everything you do as a brand — from social media outreach to content marketing efforts — must have this personal and close-connected feel to it. It's about cohesion, connection, and knock-out service.

TIPS TO STAY COMPETITIVE ON AMAZON

To say Amazon is a competitive marketplace is a litotes. In order to be successful when selling on Amazon, you need to make sure your product is noticeable to the people who might want to buy it and that your listing grabs their attention enough to make a purchase.

Invest in advertisement: High-volume seller's surely make use of Amazon sponsored ads. These ads ensure that your product is noticeable on the pages your potential buyers are already browsing. Simply put, sponsored ads gives you the chance you to purchase space at the top of Amazon search results and category listings.

Offered on a pay-per-click (PPC) system, you only pay when someone clicks on the ad. If that click converts into a sale, it can go a long way toward helping you improve your BSR and increase the visibility of your brand across the entire channel.

Use A+ pages or enhanced brand content: A+ pages and enhanced brand content (EBC) give you a greater opportunity to display your product to people who are viewing your listing.

Both of these options offer more room to describe your product and post additional pictures, allowing potential buyers a more in-depth look at your product.

This additional content provides clients with a deeper understanding of not only the product you are selling but your brand as well leading to an increased likelihood of a purchase.

Choosing A+ or EBC depends on your store sort. EBC is designed for third-party sellers and is available through Seller Central whilst A+ is for first-party sellers or vendors using Vendor Central.

TIPS TO STAY COMPETITIVE ACROSS E-COMMERCE

To be a truly fruitful high-volume seller you need to be able to move your product outside of Amazon, as well. It may be a prevalent marketplace but there are other options available that can undoubtedly increase your sales and boost your profits.

Social media also gives you the opportunity for you to grow brand awareness and trust. People are more likely to purchase from a seller they feel like they have a relationship with. By staying active online and appealing with your followers, you are amplifying this relationship.

When operating on so many channels it can be hard to keep track of customer information and which efforts you are making and where, but it is important that you try. Social media followers and their responses to your posts give you that social proof you need to convert a sale from someone who may have otherwise been sitting on the fence.

Sell on another marketplace: Increasing the number of places you sell your product can only increase the number of sales you stand to make. Amazon is massive. That's why it's an obvious place to list your products.

But no matter how much the marketplace continues to grow, it is still only part of the wider e-commerce space. And with so much competition, it makes sense to try less crowded spaces as well.

Similar to Amazon, eBay sells just about anything and has a wide-ranging customer base. If you sell handcrafted items, Etsy may be the place for you or Newegg for electronics. For every niche product, there is a niche market so do your research and list your product anywhere that makes sense.

When establishing yourself on these other channels, make sure all of your listings are different. The purpose of doing so is twofold. First, when you write a custom listing for each marketplace, you can speak directly to the customer that shops in that space. Using language that is not appropriate for the audience will alienate potential buyers and make them less likely to purchase your products.

Secondly, writing the same thing in all your listings can hurt your results in a Google search. The first result Google returns will be the most popular page. The vast majority of the time, that first hit will be your Amazon listing. Some customers will be happy to visit your Amazon listing to learn more or purchase your product but not everyone will.

If you are using different language in each listing, you increase the chances of returning multiple results on the first page and that makes it more likely that the person who initiated the search will end up clicking a link that takes them to one of your sales channels.

To be a competitive, high-volume seller, you need to use properly the tools that are available to you both on and off Amazon. Following the tips listed above may increase your brand recognition and position you to not only keep pace with the big sellers but move ahead of your direct competitors.

AMAZON COST STRATEGY

Price on Amazon is changes continuously and unless you own your private label or custom-built bundles, you need to keep your listings' prices repeatedly in order to stay in the competition. Amazon dynamic pricing helps to win Amazon buy box and to increment your sales. Employing the suitable repricing strategies for your aspirations is important, nonetheless unearthing the right ones is challenging. When selling on Amazon, you must have a united Amazon pricing strategy for backing the price you decide to charge for your items.

Here are three traditional pricing strategies you can use for your products, later we'll discuss repricing strategies.

1. Market Penetration Pricing for Amazon Startup

Also known as penetration pricing strategy, this pricing policy is mostly used by startups looking to break into the Amazon market.

What it is: Penetration pricing involves charging an amount lower than your competitors to attract customers when you're new to the Amazon world.

Initial Losses: At the beginning you can expect to cumulate some losses as your sales figures will not be big enough to cover the discount you're willing to offer to your customers. As sales grow, you can choose to stick with these sales if the general sales figure is covering costs.

Increase Prices: Most sellers don't keep their initial prices. When they think they've developed a good enough engagement with customers and have built a good standing, they usually raise their prices to match their current standing in the market.

A Warning: In the online world, charging extremely low prices usually leads customers to believe your product is of a low quality. Therefore, lower your prices by just a dollar, or a few cents, so customers don't see you suspiciously.

2. Price Skimming for Innovation

This Amazon pricing strategy is usually for those sellers who are looking to introduce something new to the amazon marketplace.

What it is: Price skimming refers to initially raising prices when you introduce a new invention or a non-existent item to the Amazon marketplace. As more players enter the market, you gradually bring down your price (while still charging more, preferably).

What it does: Charging higher prices initially means that you'll attract early adapters and lowering them eventually makes more price-conscious customers come your way. If your innovation is good enough, you can generate a lot of money by initially charging more.

Illusions: By charging an initial higher price, you will create an impression of exclusiveness and high quality. By the time competitors arrive, you'd have built a brand, already.

A Warning: Charging too high price may push customers away, even early adapters. If you have to charge a higher price, make sure your marketing for the product matches it.

3. Bundle Pricing

Bundle pricing is perhaps the most relevant for Amazonians. This Amazon pricing strategy not only do increase amazon sales, but a great way to increase visibility for your business.

What it is: It's selling multiple products together at a lower rate than what they would cost if purchased separately.

What it does: It attracts customers by making them think they are being offered something for free. You can also get rid of items that are holding inventory space and/or aren't selling well lately. Bundles work great during holiday seasons and can even increase exposure for your other products.

A Warning: if you don't offer something good to customers (something they can actually use) or include products that don't really complement each other, you'll end up generating a lot of bad PR.

Repricing Tips to Compete Amazon Dynamic Pricing

Tough competition drives sellers to reprice their items frequently in order to compete with Amazon dynamic pricing. It is not easy to continuously change the prices of your items especially when you have several products listed. In such a case, Amazon repricer tools are the best options to keep watch on competitor's and match their prices. But you can't just rely on an automated repricing software, you also need price tracker to track the prices of several competitors in order to learn about their pricing trends and history.

Take a look below on the repricing tips:

Controlling Price

Monitor Manually – Check each listing separately and modify prices as required. Doing it yourself gives you the unparalleled control, but also consume heaps of time. If you're dealing with limited number of listings, the manual handling is a good option, but in-case of large quantity it would become unworkable to do it this way.

Incorporate Automation – This basically refers to using any repricing software to automatically adjust your prices. This salvage a lot of your time and energy and even helps maintain competitiveness of your listings. However, like all other things this method isn't safe from risks as well. Keep in mind, an effective Amazon repricer not only reduce prices but also raises it, if needed.

Selecting a Repricing Strategy

Whatever pricing management mechanism you pick, it's still unavoidable to determine the price of your product. The interpretation of this will differ from seller to seller contingent upon number of aspects. Scroll down to unveil some of them.

Add Delivery in your Price Estimation

Amazon classifies listings on the basis of price delivery. For Fulfillment by Amazon program, there are no delivery charges. While pricing your products compared to other sellers, make sure you're setting it on the total cost.

Avail your FBA Benefit

If you trade through FBA, customers will usually pay extra to have a free of cost shipping advantage. Make sure to fix your rates on the basis of your FBA competition. You can even try asking for 10% more than your Merchant Fulfilled competition if you're the only FBA seller on the listing.

Select Pricing

With The Help of Amazon Price Tracker

While using an amazon price tracker for tracking prices, you can easily decide about the product price. Calculate the incurred cost of your products with fee depending on which you can fix your least possible rates.

Price isn't something that makes all the difference

Keep in mind that by just reducing your rates doesn't necessarily increase your chances of making more sales. Especially, if your product is in a low-demand niche, reducing the price will not increase your possibilities of making quick sales. One of the ways to deal with this problem is to hold your price and wait till the right customer comes up. In addition, try to include relevant keywords to the listing to optimize and improve your product visibility.

Don't post Your Strategy in Stone

Determine to opt for a flexible Amazon price strategy according to the best sellers on Amazon and don't forget every exclusive product demands unique treatment. In case you aren't content with the present results, don't be scared to try something more effective and newer.

Use Amazon Repricer Software

To effectively reprice your listings and match prices with the competition, try to put into effect Amazon repricer tool. It will help you to smoothly automate the cost changes as per your set minimum and maximum limits.

CHAPTER 6

3 SUREFIRE TIPS HOW TO CHOOSE THE BEST PRODUCTS TO PROMOTE ON AMAZON

Making money with Amazon is a very well-known method for creating a good additional online earning but if you do not know the best items to promote or how to find them, then you will issue from the beginning to make any decent money.

In the next chapter you will discover three great tips how to choose the best items to promote on Amazon

Tip 1 - Always only choose products from the bestsellers list

If you only select from items in the best sellers' category then you can be confident that those particular items already sell. Amazon is telling you that those are the hottest products in that category and people are already buying these items. This is important information and by using this single tip you will be ahead of 99% of other sellers.

Tip 2 - Always check out the product ratings and price

After you have found a product in Amazon in the best sellers' category you need to make sure there are good ratings for the product. Good being a 4 star or above as an average rating. If you only select high rated products you can be sure that customer's like the product and returns will be minimal. Also, you must make sure the product has high priced items, the higher the items the more you get paid in affiliate commissions.

Tip 3 - Always check out the product reviews

The 3rd thing you must also check for this technique to be effective are the reviews, especially   searching for how many reviews have been left for the particular product that you are looking at. A product may have a 4 or even 5 star rating but if it only has 5 reviews then it is not very convincing when people look at it and consider buying the product. The best thing to do is make sure there are a lot of reviews. A good number is around at least 50+ reviews. Also, you need to scan the whole page in the category and get an average amount of reviews, ratings and price, if the page looks good and meets these 4 pieces of criteria then you have found a great product to promote.

HOW TO BUILD YOUR BRAND ON AMAZON

There are so many sellers on Amazon, set yourself apart is key to getting ahead. You may be rolling your eyes and to overthink.

Understand What Your Brand is made of.

Before you can start building a brand, you have to know what you'll be creating. Jot down on a piece of paper the categories of products you sell, the demographics you're trying to reach, and what you want to achieve.

Build in Small Blocks

You'll want to take the same approach with building your own brand. Focus first on creating something of quality, then be patient while it'll grow (this can/will take years). Put your brand/logo on everything so that, in time, consumers will soon begin to associate it with your products.

Don't Go to Bat with the Big Boys

It can be tempting to have visions of grandeur, of competing with the likes of the world's biggest brands and products. But even if that happens (and we certainly won't discourage you of trying to reach those heights), it's going to take some serious time.

Instead, a better, smarter and more efficient strategy is to look at the really popular ideas out there, and make them your own.

Get Other People to Spread Your Word

When you first started selling on Amazon, you bought from other suppliers, suppliers with their own brands. But now that you've started to create your own brand, it's time to put the shoe on the other foot. Start soliciting to small shops to see if they can carry your brand, say yes to anyone and everyone who wants to buy in bulk from you, and set up supplier-only specials to encourage business. And think a bit outside the box, too, in trying to establish relationships with brick-and-mortar shops instead of just solely looking online.

Start squeezing Your Prices

Do you want to know one of the awe – inspiring things in dealing with your own brand? You get to cut out the intermediary, which means more money left in your pocket. And while there are a load of ways you can spend it, here's an effective one: cutting off your competition.

This technique works if your competitors are buying from already existing brands and have to pay a wholesale fee.

That way, you can merrily skip over that step and cash the money for yourself, then use it as a buffer to decrease your prices to lure more clients to you.

CHAPTER 7

4 STEPS TO FIND THE BEST AMAZON SUPPLIER FOR YOUR PRIVATE LABEL BUSINESS

You've chosen a private label product niche, and now it's the moment to find the best Amazon supplier that suits your private label business' needs.

To make your product idea come to life, finding an advisable Amazon supplier that fits your production type and is open to assembling a lasting work relation is demanding to your accomplishment as a private label auctioneer.

Here are 4 steps to find the best Amazon distributor to work with:

Step 1 – Assemble a Possible Output List

It is imperative to jot down a few product ideas and devise a list of the ones you're most attentive to. Your cultivated product search will help your fixation and registration accordingly.

Step 2 – Search for the Most Suitable Amazon Supplier

Search for Amazon suppliers by using the following resources:

Google: Start searching on Google by entering the name of the product you wish to sell followed by the term "manufacturer" or "private label supplier" as well as your location.

Alibaba: This website has a simple platform in which you can find manufacturers of various products.

Reddit: Many seller focused subreddits are incredibly active. Search for posts related to your product(s) and look for manufacturers there.

Amazon/eBay: You can check out the manufacturers' names for the products you're most interested in; however, it should be noted that Amazon may be more saturated than other platforms, so it may not be the best choice to find low competition products. Search eBay for products you're interested in to dig up more supplier options.

Indiamart: Similar to Alibaba, you can find all types of household, sport, tool, apparel, accessory products, and more.

Global Sources: This is another great source to find private label suppliers that can import for less than many US-made goods.

Attend Trade Shows Abroad: There are trade shows around the world each year that show off the work of different manufacturers and offer a chance to speak with a representative personally to get a true sense of how the supplier functions.

Step 3 – Assess Potential Amazon Suppliers

Having some basic guidelines in mind when assessing potential manufacturers will make it easier for you to find the right supplier.

As you explore various suppliers and speak with them, consider the following factors:

Price

Find out the cost of the raw materials needed for your product, average labor wages, and other manufacturing costs typical of your kind of product, then compare with the supplier's proposed pricing to see if it is fair and not exorbitant.

Reliability

Large suppliers tend to be more reliable due to their well-structured systems and well-trained staff to serve many clients at once.

Small suppliers can often provide more individualized attention, foster stronger relationships, and give you a stronger sense of prioritization.

Retention rate, especially after Lunar New Year celebrations when workers often do not return to work, should play a crucial role in your decision since skilled workers are not easily replaced and can lower the quality of your product.

Versatility

If you're considering new product launches in the near future, find out the supplier's capabilities in producing different products concurrently.

Stability/Competency

- How long has the manufacturer been in business?
- What do customers say about this manufacturer?
- How is the company's overall reputation?

- Does the manufacturer keep up with the latest products and services?
- Does the company provide excellent customer service?

Location

- How close is the supplier to you?
- How close is the supplier to the nearest sea freight port or airport?
- How close is the supplier is to your desired fulfillment centers?

Government Compliance

Ensure that the manufacturer's production facility is compliant with government regulations and environmental precautions with a third-party inspection company; independent inspectors will often provide detailed reports without bias on the state of the manufacturer's facility.

Step 4 – Request a quote and Sample Products

Once you've narrowed your choices down to a chosen few Amazon suppliers, it's time to request a quote. The quote should include the following items:

- Private label and packaging fees – Some Amazon suppliers will charge for starting a new private label and packaging your products
- Shipping fees to your fulfillment location
- Product prices for quantities ordered
- Import requirements and/or duties that must be met or paid

Afterwards, you will want to demand sample products so that you know what kind of traits the Amazon supplier can administer.

Most suppliers will implement you with a sample at a low cost. Study the sample and make notes as to how it can be enhanced if the supplier has at least proven itself to craft a quality product. If you are unsatisfied overall, you may be better off looking at another Amazon supplier. If you're serious about having your own private label, this will be a worthwhile initial expenditure.

CHAPTER 8

HOW TO PREPARE AND LIST PRODUCTS IN AMAZON

Once you've explored, found and purchased products to sell on Amazon, you're only an inch away from making your first sale. Listing products on Amazon lawfully makes them available to millions of people across the world. Before listing products, you need to gather some information about them. There are two methods to list your products on Amazon: individual or bulk.

How to List Amazon items Individually

Listing products individually is advised when starting out. It gives sellers a better idea of information is behind each product. To start listing items, visit the inventory tab of Seller Central, and click "Add an Item." You will be showed a search bar and the option to create a new item. The easiest way to do this is entering noticeable information within the search bar and searching Amazon's catalog for the item information. If you find your item, there is definitely an option to sell yours.

The three required pieces of information to list your items are item condition, price, and item quantity. You may also indicate sale date and prices, restock dates, and select shipping items. Lastly, you can create a SKU for your product, which is a unique identifier for managing your products. Amazon creates one for you if you don't specify one.

The "Create a New Product Tool" is used if you're unable to find your item After selecting the button, browse to the category that your item best fits under. Keep in mind that some items require approval from Amazon before they can be sold; for example, jewelry or automotive parts. The "Create a Product" page requires more details than if you were to find it in Amazon's catalog. This is to make sure you provide a complete listing for buyers. You are required to fill in the manufacturer, product name, and UPC of the product. The UPC is necessary because it helps buyers identify products easier, even if you've accidentally mislabeled them.

Take a Picture of Your Amazon Product

Uploading pictures of the product is paramount, because buyers usually won't make a purchase without seeing the product. On this page is a drop-down box labeled "Variation Theme." This gives sellers the ability to list products of different colors or slightly varied designs without listing them one-by-one. You will need a picture of each variant listed.

How to List Items in Bulk on Amazon

The ability to list items in bulk is a convenience for Amazon sellers who have large inventories. Amazon provides templates of various types of stores. For example, a clothing-related store would require the clothing template. If you have existing inventory that you listed individually or any time previously, its recommended that you make sure that all the information for those products is entered correctly. If it needs changes, you can do that in one step while you're listing new items.

If there is existing inventory, select everything and then "Export to File" under the action tab. If you don't select all items, your store will be incomplete when you update your inventory. Copy all existing items to the template, and add new items as well. Once this is done, upload the new inventory file under "Manage Inventory" in Seller Central.

BRANDED SCANNERS AT AMAZON

A scanner is a device which is used for the purpose of scanning images, objects, printing text, hand writing, certificates and other such kind of material. Scanners are widely used in offices to scan their important documents in order to keep record of the activities performed in an organization. These scanners convert the scanned image into digital form which could be then saved in the computer for further use. Most of the people use branded scanners for their personal and office use, as they are not only efficient but rather effective as well.

Amazon also offers a huge variety of branded scanner including Fujitsu, Epson, Cannon and a lot of other branded scanners. The scanners offered by Amazon can be seen on their website along with their picture, specification and cost. In addition, differentiation of different kinds of scanners in term of their cost & qquality is also very easy because all of them are exposed on the website of Amazon along with the required details.

Buyers can not only buy new scanner but also used scanners are offered by Amazon. Buyer can also pick their favorite brand from the website which will then expose all the models offered by the selected brand.

CHAPTER 9

WHY BRAND SHOULD FOCUS ON AMAZON ADVERTISING

Different factors come into play when trying to file your products in Amazon search.

Also, Amazon has been constrained reviews and rank manipulation.

To accommodate a lot of marketing energy that was hitherto focused on gathering reviews has shifted to advertising on Amazon.

Instead of focusing on discounted products for reviews – or, even worse, encourage reviews – you can use Amazon Advertising to start initial conversions.

This leads to product reviews as your sales velocity increases.

This allows you to get the traffic and conversions you need for your product to be ranked organically.

When working with products on Amazon, the ranking problem is solved by combining Amazon advertising with different promotional offerings that Amazon offers (e.g., clippable coupons).

Initially, after launching a product, you will heavily rely on Amazon advertising to rank your product on the first page.

However, if your product is optimized correctly, your reliance on Amazon advertising will decrease with time.

Nevertheless, you might still need to carry on some advertising even after your products have ranked high to protect your digital real estate or from competitor's who might still be using Amazon advertising.

The more niche your product is, the less you will likely have to spend on advertising on Amazon's platform.

However, for most products, I have found that at present the cost to advertise on Amazon is significantly less than other advertising platforms like Google Ads.

Should You Advertise on Amazon?

If you already have a product that can sell online, then you can advertise on Amazon.

Amazon offers you a way to get your product in front of shoppers at a much lower cost than competing advertising platforms.

You can start with a product that already sells well and measures your ROI before adding other products.

Over the last several years, Amazon Advertising has had a variety of changes, and recently, they renamed some of their products.

Here are four ways to advertise on Amazon.

1. Sponsored Products

This is the most popular method of advertising on Amazon.

Brands have used this powerful tool for many years to automatically and manually target shoppers.

Here, you can use different match types that are familiar to you as an advertiser – broad, phrase and exact match, as well as negative keyword matching.

Any seller on Amazon Seller Central, Kindle Direct Publishing, or Vendor Central platform can participate in the Sponsored Products program.

Amazon has been rolling out additional targeting options on its Seller Central platform such as Product, Interest, and Category Targeting.

It is rumored that even more match types might be available to advertisers in the near future.

While the match types mimic Google's advertising platforms, there are some nuances to Sponsored Products.

Before setting up your campaign, check the following to make sure that your campaign will run:

Own the Buy-Box

Your ad will not run if you do not have the buy box for that product.

This means if a brand is selling a product directly and there are third-party sellers in the buy box, the brand will be unable to run any Sponsored Products Ads for that product.

Amazon SEO Tips to Boost Your Listings and Sales

Amazon accounts for 43% of all online sales. This retail giant is one of the largest and fastest growing retailers on the web. Many businesses sell products on Amazon, so if you want to help your business stand out and reach more customers, you need to use Amazon search engine optimization (SEO).

How does Amazon SEO work?

Before we dive into our Amazon SEO tips, it's important to understand how Amazon ranks products. The way people search on Amazon is different than Google, so there is a slight learning curve.

When people search for products on Amazon, they can only find your products if their search queries match your keywords. This creates a challenge because you must use keywords that your audience uses to find products like yours.

The important thing to note is that Amazon's A9 algorithm focuses on displaying products first that increase purchase likelihood. The algorithm focuses on two factors: performance and relevance. Performance is based on how well your products sell and relevance is based on how your keyword match the search query.

Therefore, keyword selection is challenging. It isn't enough to choose the right keywords to get your products to rank. You need to offer products that consumers will want to buy or one that consumers already buy frequently.

Amazon thinks about the buyers. They want to expose products that best fit their queries. When you optimize your listings, you need to base on the buyer's experience and how you can make it even better.

6 TIPS FOR IMPROVING YOUR AMAZON SEO

If you want your market to find your products, you need to improve your Amazon rankings. It will help you reach more valuable leads that are focused in your products.

1. Conduct keyword research

If you've used SEO before, you probably know about conducting keyword research. With Amazon SEO, keyword research has some similar qualities to traditional SEO, but with a few more buyer-focused qualities.

Just like traditional SEO, you want to focus on long-tail keywords. These are keywords that contain three or more words. When people search for products on Amazon, they use long-tail keywords to find products.

Long-tail keywords will help more interested leads find your product listings. It is important that you focus on all relevant keywords. You don't want to miss out on potential leads because you didn't include certain keywords in your Amazon product listings.

To help you figure out the right keywords for your Amazon SEO campaign, you can use a free tool called Sonar. This is a keyword research tool that focuses specifically on keywords that people use on Amazon. It helps you see the search volume for each keyword, which enables you to prioritize them in your Amazon SEO campaign.

Once you select your keywords, you need to integrate them into your listings. You need to use them in places like the product titles and descriptions. This will help your products appear in search results for those keywords.

2. Manage your reviews

Reviews are a crucial part of any business. They can be the reason a person buys your products or decides to pass. It is important that you manage product reviews to help improve your Amazon SEO campaign.

For the most part, the products in the top of Amazon's search results generally have four or more stars. These are products that have great reviews and people enjoy. You want to encourage your audience to leave feedback about their experience with your products.

When your audience leaves feedback, there's a good chance you'll receive negative reviews. As part of managing your reviews, you need to take the time to respond to negative reviews. It will prevent you from deterring future customers.

Your response to negative reviews allows people to see how you handle negativity. If you address the issues, offer to replace broken or damaged products, and respond to questions, you'll encourage more people to buy your products. They will feel more confident that your company takes issues seriously and that if they have an issue with your products, they know you will respond.

This will lead to more conversions and positive reviews. It will improve your rankings in Amazon search results.

3. Optimize your title

The way you format your title will affect where you appear in the search results. It's important that you include all vital elements into your title.

The general format to create a product title is:

This is the general rule of thumb for how to order your title. These categories may not all apply to your products, but you want to use the ones that do. The order of your title impacts how your audience finds your listings, so it is important that you stick to the proper order.

When you optimize your title, you want to place your most relevant keyword first. This ensures that people always see your most important keyword, regardless of how short or long the title appears in the search results. It also helps your listings appear in the most relevant search results.

4. Follow image guidelines

Images play a vital role in the purchasing process. People need to see products from different angles to get a better sense of how the products look. It's a key component to help build confidence and trust with your audience — especially since they can't physically see the product in front of them.

Amazon encourages you to use product images that are larger than 1000x1000 pixels. This is because they have a zoom feature that allows users to zoom in one image when they are above that dimension. If you want to provide a more positive experience for your audience, you need to use images that are larger than the dimension stated before.

The ability to zoom in can possibly increase sales for your business. People can look at your items more in-depth and get a better sense of how they look. It becomes even more helpful when you post multiple photos with different angles where an audience possibly use the different zooming characteristics.

Adding zoomable images doesn't directly affect your Amazon SEO, but it does improve your conversion rate. When you earn more conversions, you increase your listing's ranking. It can also help you earn more reviews, which also impacts in a positive way your product listing's performance.

5. Think about your price

Pricing is an important factor for customers. They want to get the best product and spend less. When you expose your product on Amazon, you need to look at how your competitors' pricing.

If you're selling your product for $100 and all your competitors have a similar product for $20 - $30, you won't help your Amazon SEO campaign. In fact, your product list won't rank because it is too expensive. Your audience will choose a cheaper product that suites their needs.

To have competitive listings, you need to see how your competitors are pricing products similar to yours. This will help you get a better idea of how to price your product and see if your product can even compete amongst the competition.

6. Use bullet points in your item descriptions

When you post a new product, you probably have a lot you want to say about to describe it. After all, you really want to sell your public to beneficial your products compared to the competitors. When you do this, it is vital that you break down your information so it is manageable for your public to read.

The best way to do this is to divide your product descriptions into bullet points. It's an easy way for your public to digest the information. People like when information is short and easy to read.

Products with bullet points usually convert better, as well. People read the information more and feel more informed to buy. This helps improve your Amazon SEO ranking because you get more conversions.

CHAPTER 10

HOW TO LAUNCH A NEW PRODUCT ON AMAZON

Even if you're a first-time private label seller on Amazon or are already established and looking to improve launching a new product takes time and careful planning. After all, you don't want to end up investing all your resources in a new item that doesn't sell or give you high allowances. You rather want something that will win you the Buy Box and set your private label business on a path for long-term production.

To help you get there, follow these five advises for launching a new item on Amazon:

1. Choose an alluring Product & Price

It goes without saying that you want to sell a product that will actually, well, sell. If you've been selling on Amazon for a while, you likely have an idea of what's in demand. But in case you need a refresher or if this is your first time selling do some research. You can look on Amazon (or even Alibaba) to see what the top-selling products are or consult a product research tool to do the heavy lifting for you.

Once you decide on what you're going to sell, you have two price-points to think about: the sourcing cost and the selling price. For the former, you want to pay the lowest possible price to have your product made — that means comparison shopping and negotiating with suppliers. For the latter, you want a price that will attract sales, win you the Buy Box, and give you high margins — that means researching competitors prices, looking up the price history for a similar product and/or using a repricer tool.

Your last step here is to create a stellar product detail page that includes everything a customer needs to familiarize themselves with your product: high-resolution images, product demos, accurate and thorough descriptions, etc.

2. Manage Your Inventory/Supply Chain

Once you've chosen your product and price, you need to stock up so you can avoid a stockout. That means developing an inventory management strategy to determine how much product to order at the start plus how much to have on hand at any given time in the future.

Understanding this information will not only prevent you from running out of stock, it will also keep you from buying too much at one time. Not only that, you'll know when and how much to reorder as business picks up.

As important as it is to manage your inventory, it is fairly important to be on top of the supply chain as well. That way, you can establish the reorder process and not run up against any surprises or delays when it's time to place a new order. Nonetheless establish an agreement with your suppliers and stay in frequent communication with them — i.e. don't just reach out when you need more items.

3. Create rumors

Generate interest in your items before it's actually listed so that when your listing is actually live, you don't have to work as hard to get clients. You can do this by advertising its release on social media or your own website if you may have one.

Then chase the pre-release marketing with a Sponsored Product campaign on Amazon. To really create a lot of "rumors", you can offer a new special item or for example a discount for the first 150 customers.

4. Create Reviews

Since online shoppers can't preview or test your items in person, they trust on feedback from previous customers before making a purchase decision. But you can't consequently launch a new product with reviews. Unless, that is, you have a separate ecommerce channel you can launch on first.

In other words, if you have your own ecommerce website, consider launching their first and running a marketing campaign on social media and other channels outside of Amazon. From there, you can solicit feedback from your customers and build up reviews on your website.

Then, use those reviews in your marketing campaigns for the Amazon launch, directing people to your Amazon listing. After your Amazon launch and as you start making sales, you can solicit feedback from your Amazon customers.

5. Get money

Initiate a new item isn't cheap, especially when it's a private label product. After all, you have packaging and branding expenses to budget for in addition to anything else.

Find the best Amazon Bargains – 4 Secrets to saving up to 65% on Amazon

Amazon has always been a main player in the e-commerce industry. There are a huge variety of items categories listed on their website, with available products numbering in the millions. Along with all these items come several ways to save money while shopping on Amazon. We'll look at a few of these methods and see just how easy it is to save money and find Amazon deals.

Amazon Discount Codes

Amazon sometimes provides coupon codes that you can apply to your purchases to save money. Although these are not regularly advertised by Amazon, a quick Internet search will reveal a plethora of coupons. One of the great things about these discounts is that they are deducted from the total price of your shopping cart. This will sometimes allow you to get free shipping on items which cost less than $25. Amazon coupon codes usually apply to certain products or categories only.

When you find a coupon code for a product you are interested in, all you do is enter it in the "Promotional Codes" box when you're checking out. The discount will then be applied directly to your shopping cart and you'll see the savings instantaneously.

Cash Back Rewards

Another way to save money on Amazon is by using their new Platinum credit card. This will allow you to save money on every purchase you make. For every dollar you spend at Amazon you will obtain three points on your card. These points can be accumulated and transformed into Amazon gift certificates which you can use towards your purchases. For every 2500 points you collect, Amazon will provide you with a gift certificate valued at $25. If you do the math, it turns out you get about 3% cash back on all your purchases. This is a great reward especially considering most other cards only give you 1% cash back. On top of that, your first purchase with the card will receive an immediate $30 discount. All the gift certificates you earn with the card can be used during your checkout process.

Free Shipping Offer

One of the fantastic things about Amazon is its Super Saver Shipping. What this means is that most items purchased directly from Amazon or from one of its third-party retailers are eligible for free shipping as long as the order total is over $25. Although the Super Saver Shipping is generally slower than other shipping methods available on Amazon, in our experience orders still arrive very quickly. Because the shipping costs on many online purchases can normally be quite expensive, this is a fantastic way to save money.

Amazon Price History Tracker / Price Drop Alerts

Another excellent way to find Amazon deals is by being aware of upcoming sales. If you are like many other people and lead a hectic life, this can normally prove to be a very difficult task. Fortunately, there are Amazon price tracking tools available which will keep an eye out for sales on your behalf, and alert you when prices drop. How does this work exactly?

Well, suppose you are looking to purchase a new color printer. You would visit a price tracking website and enter the name of the printer you wanted into the search box. This would bring up a list of printers available on Amazon. You could then set up a price drop alert for the particular printer you are interested in and the price tracking website would send you an e-mail the next time that printer goes on sale. This is a brilliant way to save loads of money on those big-ticket items you're saving up for.

Adding it all up

Now that we have explored some of the ways to save money on Amazon, let's take a look at a real-world example of how much you can save. Suppose that color printer you are looking to purchase normally sells for $300. The first step would be to track the price of the printer on an Amazon price history tracking website. When the printer goes on a 1-day sale for 50% off (which you'll be alerted to immediately, lucky you!), the price drops down to $150. Next, doing a quick Internet search we'll see that there is a $25 coupon code available for all color printers on Amazon. Using this coupon code along with free shipping and 3% cash back (obtained when using the Amazon Platinum credit card), here's what the savings would look like:

- Normal retail price is $300.
- Get it at 50% off by setting up a price drop alert. Subtract $150.
- Subtract $25 using the Amazon discount code.
- Subtract $30 with the first purchase on an Amazon Platinum credit card.
- Subtract $2.85 for the 3% cash back.
- Get free shipping on orders over $25.
- The total: $92.15 - a total savings of 70% off the retail price!

Obviously, if you make a lot of purchases on Amazon these savings will really add up. Fortunately for us, Amazon makes it really simple to save money. It's just one of the many ways they like to reward their valued customers.

COMMON MISTAKES TO AVOID WHEN SHOPPING WITH COUPONS

Coupons are supposed to make you incredible savings on your purchases. However, if you are not wise with how you use the coupons, you could end up making little payoffs. Shoppers who hunt for coupons to make the big savings on items need to come out with some sort of strategy to ensure they get maximum deals possible with the coupons they have. If you are among shoppers that like enjoying discounts using coupons, here are some errors you should try and avoid if at all you want to enjoy maximum benefits using the coupons.

Mistake 1 - Sticking to one brand

To enjoy great savings with your coupons, you really do not have the luxury of being loyal to a particular brand. Sure, you may love the brand for a number of reasons, but you will not save much if you choose to stick only to products from that brand. If you are really inclined to making savings, then do not let great deals pass you by just because you prefer a particular brand over another.

Mistake 2 - Buying any item on sale

As much as items on sale offer even better returns when using coupons, not every one of those items will be a good sale for you. Evaluate what is in the sale for you so you can decide to go ahead or to wait for a much better sale that offers you greater value with the coupon. It is not always worth to use coupons on every item on sale because it may not save you much in the end. Do your calculations and choose the most rewarding sales.

Mistake 3 - Using coupons on items that are full priced

Whereas coupons are supposed to make items you want more affordable by saving you some money, you will enjoy greater price cuts when you use them on items that are on sale rather than on items that are full-priced. When you use coupons on items that are on sale, you end up getting the items almost free, but when you choose to use on full priced items, then you only manage to save a few coins on them. Whenever possible, try not to use coupons on full priced items and instead look for sales on items you are in need of.

Mistake 4 - Using Every coupon you find

Not all coupons represent real savings and you consequently do not have to take advantage of every coupon that you find. A good coupon is one that offers you real discounts on items that you really need. So instead of picking up any coupon you find along, access its value first and determine that it is worth. You should also only use the coupon on items you really will use and not just any item you can enjoy the markdown on. It does not make any sense to be hurried in using coupons on products you never use or will never end up using otherwise you end up wasting a possible good offer.

CHAPTER 11

HOW TO HIT YOUR TARGET ACOS ON AMAZON

ACoS on itself is just a number. In order to optimize your Ads and increase your margins, you need to understand how it works and what it means in practically.

What does it mean a low vs. high acos?

The lower your ACoS is the better your Ad is working: a theoretical ACoS of zero would mean you spend nothing, yet make a sale.

A high ACoS means an underperforming Ad. You are spending more to reach your target audience and are in danger of losing margins on your Ad.

But just how low or high must your ACoS be?

How to figure the right acos for your ad campaign

In order to determine the right ACoS for your Ad campaign, you need to first understand what Break-Even ACoS and Target ACoS are.

Break-Even ACoS is the point where an Ad neither makes nor loses money. Any ACoS lower than your Break-Even

ACoS is profitable. Conversely, any ACoS higher than that is costing you money.

Of course, merely breaking even is rarely an advertiser's goal, unless used as a short-term strategy—for example, to raise brand awareness. What you normally want is to make a profit?

Your Ad's profitability is determined by the Target ACoS. This is your ideal ACoS—how much your profit should be for a particular product. If your Break-Even ACoS gives you an upper limit above which your Ad is no longer profitable, your Target ACoS lets you know how profitable an Ad is.

Break-Even ACoS and Target ACoS are the keys to determining the right ACoS for your Ad campaign:

Any ACoS lower than your Target ACoS further increases your profit margin.

Any ACoS higher than your Target ACoS but lower than your Break-Even ACoS is profitable, but eats into your profits.

And any ACoS higher than your Break-Even ACoS is making a loss.

How to measure profit with acos

To better understand how ACoS can help you calculate your profit, you need to remember that your Break-Even ACoS depends on a number of factors beyond your Ad campaigns' cost.

How to lower your acos

Most advertisers start a campaign with the goal of reaching the Break-Even point. They then optimize toward their Target ACoS.

In practice, this means you need to lower your Ad's cost while increasing its profitability. This is a continuing process which can take weeks—or even months of optimization.

There are many factors which can impact on your success with reaching your Target ACoS, only some of which are within your control. For example, your ACoS depends on your target audience, the market your product belongs to, who your competitors are, and how much they are investing on AMS. You can't control any of these.

However, there are also a number of things you can control in order to improve your campaign's success and optimize your Amazon ACoS.

The Importance of Ad Ranking

The first thing to do when striving to reach your Target ACoS is to put yourself in Amazon's shoes. Amazon prides itself on its customer-centric approach, so the company prioritizes a relevant and helpful shopping experience for their customers. They want to ensure that their search results are helpful and that any advertising shown will improve their shopping experience instead of being an irritation.

Furthermore, a successful Ad is also in the company's interest in other ways as well. The company makes its money in two ways:

- By selling you advertising space on its pages, and
- By taking a percentage of each sale.

WHAT IS AMAZON PRODUCT ATTRIBUTE TARGETING?

The Amazon Product Targeting is the newest targeting mechanism that allows you to build a targeted campaign based on the characteristics of the target product you are able to specify.

In simple words, the Product Targeting Beta allows you to set your Amazon ads to appear on other people's ASIN pages and the category search results.

It allows refined targeting options to display your product ads alongside other product ASINs, brands, categories with refinements in the price, brand, and ratings.

Product Attribute Targeting is twofold,

1. Manual Product Targeting with granular refinements
2. Enhanced Automatic Targeting Options

Best Strategies to employ with Product Attribute Targeting

1. Maximized Attention for a Product Launch or for Increasing Brand Awareness.

A new product launch could do good with a lot of visibility. Especially since it's a new launch it's hard to predict what keywords could work the best.

The main aim during the launch phase is to generate the maximum sales during this period, product targeting can be an advantage to target popular brands and similar products, while you benefit from their visibility.

This strategy could be a great benefit for products with upgraded and reinvented features from the existing products. Eg. If you have invented a better sunscreen, it makes sense to target the top-selling sunscreen brand.

2. Explore into Competitors' Market Space

The most obvious use of Product Targeting is to attack your competitors and capture sales.

Do thorough research before you target products. Look through your Automatic campaign Search Term report to discover ASINs you are converting the most. Think twice before targeting a better product that has better ratings or a lower price than yours.

3. Defend your Market Share

Remember, just like you, your competitors are also going to take advantage of the product targeting ads. So, build brand awareness by showcasing your entire product line by targeting your own products.

Targeting your own product will ensure that buyers will not stray towards your competitors' products

Direct the most attention to products that have good ratings, reviews, are lower priced, which could be tough for your competitors to steal from.

94

While advertising your products against your other products, ensure that you pair products that are a good buy with the targeted product.

Understanding the Manual Product Attribute Targeting types

Amazon allows sellers to choose the target where you want your ads to appear by choosing the targeting option from the following.

1. Category Targeting
2. Individual ASIN Targeting

1. Category Targeting

This is where you can target a category of products as a whole. The category can be chosen from the search bar and also by the brand name, price range and the review rating.

Word of Caution: Since this option allows targeting the entire category of products that are of relevance to your product, it can be leveraged as advantage by-products that fall into the are frequently bought together and by brands trying to build brand awareness.

Brainstorm and carefully consider product categories that could be your best target audience. For each category that's selected, refine the category to target products based on a particular brand, price range, and star rating to choose the best target.

2. Individual Product Targeting

In the products tab, you can target suggested individual products that are similar to your products or search/upload specific ASINs.

Category targeting VS Individual ASIN targeting – When and what to use

The Category Targeting is a nice way to get a lot of visibility, a benefit when you are trying to build brand recognition or a product launch. Nevertheless since you are eligible for a broad reach, the ad is likely to show up on a lot of searches, resulting in a lower conversion rate, with a high ACoS unless you have an faultless brand with a very desirable product having chosen the right set of categories.

The Individual Product Targeting is a much restricted reach compared to the former, nevertheless it is a more mature way of targeting products since you are likely to choose items at which point you stand an upper hand in winning the sale, or products that are trying to eat up your space in the marketplace.

CHAPTER 12

WHICH FULFILLMENT OPTION IS BETTER FOR AMAZON SELLERS?

If you're an Amazon seller, one of your most important decisions will be whether or not you ship using Fulfillment by Amazon (FBA), Merchant Fulfilled Network (MFN, or sometimes FBM, as in "fulfillment by merchant"), or even both.

Amazon sellers have strong opinions about each method, and each has its own points of strengths and weaknesses.

FBA vs MFN: What's the difference?

Sellers who use FBA pay fees to store their products in Amazon's fulfillment centers as well as for Amazon's world-class fulfillment services.

When an order is placed for a seller's FBA product, Amazon receives the information, picks the stock from the shelves, packs it, and ships it.

Amazon also provides the customer service for all FBA products. These services are covered by Amazon's FBA fulfillment fees, which are based on the size and weight of items sold. Amazon also imposes short- and long-term storage fees, so the longer an item stays in FBA inventory, the more fees a seller will incur.

MFN simply refers to sellers shipping their own products directly from their own homes, businesses, or warehouses after receiving orders through Amazon.com.

This means that locating the stock, packing the orders, arranging the shipping, and providing all customer service is the direct responsibility of the seller.

There's also Seller Fulfilled Prime (SFP), a relatively new fulfillment option that awards MFN sellers with excellent metrics. Those who qualify for Amazon SFP enjoy the benefits of FBA without having to send shipments to Fulfillment Centers.

Amazon SFP sellers also seem to get the same royal treatment as FBA sellers from Amazon's Buy Box algorithm. That means stellar sellers with their own fulfillment systems in place can win the Buy Box just as often as FBA sellers pending their seller metrics remain high across the board without having to incur FBA fees.

Advantages of using FBA vs MFN

There are many advantages to using FBA, especially for sellers with high margins who can absorb Amazon's ever-evolving FBA fees.

One major FBA perk is that you become eligible to offer Prime shipping to your customers. On top of being able to tap into Amazon Prime customers, you'll also increase your odds of winning the Buy Box because "fulfillment method" has heavy weight in Amazon's algorithm, with preference given to FBA listings.

As an FBA seller, you can offer all of the shipping options that Amazon does, no matter the size of your business. You also gain access to Amazon's remarkably efficient shipping and distribution network, along with access to Amazon's discounted shipping rates.

Faster shipping especially pleases Amazon Prime customers, who are accustomed to taking advantage of free Prime 2-day shipping.

Another FBA advantage is that many Amazon customers know what they want and are willing to pay for it. According to Amazon, almost half of their customer base refuses to buy from seller's who do not use FBA. This makes sense, considering that not just shipping, but also customer service, are so important to those who subscribe to Prime.

Using FBA vs MFN is a way that even the smallest sellers can set themselves apart from the competition. You'll be listed higher in Amazon search and be more likely to have your listings chosen by customers.

Cons of using FBA

As any FBA seller will tell you, the major disadvantage to FBA is the cost. Because Amazon holds all the cards, the company can tack on as many fees for its service as it deems appropriate.

As long as FBA remains a cheaper fulfillment option than MFN for a large portion of sellers, Amazon can continue increasing FBA fees.

Amazon also charges long-term inventory storage fees for sluggish products. These fees are an effort to discourage sellers from shipping stagnant inventory to FBA Fulfillment Centers that take up precious inventory space.

Pros and cons to fulfilling via Amazon MFN

One clear advantage for MFN sellers is that they can ensure their packaging is perfect for their products. This leads to fewer damaged products being reported by customers, and, as a result, fewer returns.

MFN sellers can also create custom packaging to differentiate their Amazon store from competitors. To take this even further, MFN sellers can create custom receipts and even include hand-written thank-you notes to customers.

Of course, having to handle the packaging and shipping is a clear disadvantage to using MFN. Worse yet, MFN sellers have to deal with customer service issues and returns. These are time-consuming and, at times, difficult tasks, and the fees paid to FBA is often worth it.

The other main disadvantage to MFN is that buyers aren't always as happy to use it. How much this impacts your business isn't always clear, but Prime users spend more than non-Prime shoppers on average. And, they also tend to purchase Prime products over non-Prime ones; that's what they're paying for, after all.

Using MFN may also decrease your chances of winning the Buy Box versus FBA competitors.

Some sellers test each fulfillment method with limited inventory using both MFN and FBA listings so they can see which works better for them. Sometimes, MFN and FBA fulfillment have different advantages for the same seller, depending on the products being sold.

For example, if there is a particular packaging issue for or a target buyer who isn't picky about shipping speed, MFN may be a better option. And, for heavy or bulky items, sellers may also prefer fulfilling via MFN so they don't have to incur extra shipping fees.

On the other hand, FBA would work better for high-volume Amazon sellers who can't afford to spend time (or money hiring staff) to handle packing and shipping an excess of orders.

The typical seller that would benefit from FBA vs MFN

Amazon sellers poised to make the most of MFN are those who already have storage and shipping systems in place. If you've got a warehouse (or several), staff, and a logistics network you trust, consider using MFN and reaping higher profit margins.

Better yet, if you have exceptional seller metrics, apply for Amazon Seller Fulfilled Prime and enjoy the benefits of FBA without paying FBA fees.

If you have an operational eCommerce website or a brick and mortar store, you're also in a much better position to successfully fulfill orders. If you can handle it, you'll save yourself a fortune in storage and fulfillment fees.

On the other side, if your business can't rapidly and effectively fill orders, FBA is probably the better option.

Small-time sellers can benefit from FBA since many buyer's actively look for stores with items that feature Prime shipping.

Bigger sellers can also benefit from FBA by strategically fulfilling orders with MFN and then using FBA on listings where it makes more sense. And any seller that lists items with high sales velocity can benefit from FBA, as they'll avoid getting hit with long-term storage fees.

CHAPTER 13

HOW TO GET A LOAN TO START AN AMAZON FBA BUSINESS

It wasn't so long ago that starting a retail business would cost tens of thousands, at least. You needed pay rent for store, hire staff and pay thousands in manufacturing just to start.

In 2006, Amazon revolutionized small business with Fulfillment by Amazon (FBA) and now anyone can initiate their own brand and sell it to the world. Starting an Amazon FBA business costs a fraction of what you'd pay to launch a traditional business and you've got the world's biggest ecommerce website in your corner.

The opportunity is incredibly amazing. Amazon FBA sellers report an average profit of 66% and monthly sales of $10,000 or more between 18 months. Even smaller sellers can make a few bucks a month within the first year of business.

While costs to start an Amazon store are much lower, they can still run into the thousands. Even with the reseller strategy, costs can reach $2,000 to start your business.

How Much Does It Cost to Start an Amazon FBA Business?

Starting an Amazon FBA business isn't as inexpensive as starting a website or some of the other work-at-home businesses. Then again, you wouldn't expect to be able to start your own retail brand with just a few hundred dollars.

Even so, starting an ecommerce business through Amazon is still millions cheaper than the traditional route of renting commercial space and buying all the manufacturing inputs necessary to a private-label brand. This is the real opportunity in Amazon FBA, to be able to compete with the biggest brands and get started for just a few thousand.

Let's walk through the costs of getting started on Amazon FBA as a private-label first then as a reseller of other products.

I like the private-label business model because you can create some real brand strength in your products and grow your business. The reseller model means you're always on that hamster wheel of buying and selling.

Manufacturing costs for a new Amazon FBA Business – Manufacturing is by far your biggest cost with an Amazon FBA business. This goes for startup costs as well as ongoing production. Sites like Alibaba make it easy to connect with low-cost, Chinese manufacturers that can provide consistent quality but it's still going to cost some money.

Your first step here is to find a manufacturer and order samples. There are hundreds of providers on Alibaba for every product and quality can vary quite a bit even from what is listed on the website. Research at least three manufacturers to send you a test sample of the product. This is usually going to cost a nominal fee of $100 per sample but is well worth it to find a reliable producer.

Once you've chosen your Amazon supplier, you'll need to order initial inventory. You'll get discounts for ordering in bulk and most manufacturers have a minimum order quantity (MOq). Don't be intimidated by a minimum order that means putting down a few thousand. This is your biggest expense and can be hugely profitable if you've done your planning beforehand.

The average product sold on Amazon FBA costs around $20 and can usually be manufactured for less than $5 each. Ordering a batch of 500 for your initial inventory means costs of $2,500 to start your FBA business.

That means producer testing and inventory will cost you around $3,000 to get started. Note that these are estimated costs for a small product costing roughly $5 to manufacture, package and ship to Amazon's FBA warehouses.

You can relax now that the biggest cost is out of the way. It gets easier on the budget from here.

Photography and Video: You'll need professional images for your product and a video demonstration can really help your marketing efforts. I'd recommend looking on Craigslist for these services but make sure you check out a few providers and their past work. You can get all the photos you need plus a couple of short 45-second videos for $500 or less.

Amazon Professional Account: You can sell your FBA products through an individual account but it costs about $1 per item. Starting an Amazon Professional account costs $40 a month but you don't pay the per item fees. Hopefully, you're planning on selling more than 40 items a month so the professional account makes more sense.

With the professional account, you also get bonus features like promotional codes and better tracking.

UPC Code for your product: You need a barcode, a Global Trade Identification Number (GTIN) for each product you sell. Many Amazon FBA businesses are still using third-party UPC codes even though Amazon has change their requirements stating you need a code from GS1.

It's more expensive at $250 for registration and a $50 annual renewal for up to 10 barcodes but go the safe route and stay in compliance. The last thing you want to do is go through all this work only to get your store shut down by Amazon.

Amazon Marketing: Next to manufacturing, marketing is your next biggest expense and may even be a bigger cost for some products. Amazon doesn't disclose how many FBA stores there are but the world's largest ecommerce platform ships more than a billion sales every year. So yeah, that's a lot of competition no matter what's your product.

You can market your product through Facebook, Twitter or your own website but the best marketing channel for most FBA businesses is through sponsored ads directly on Amazon. That's where your potential customers are most ready and willing to buy.

Once sales and reviews start coming in, your product will rank on Amazon and your business will have a life of its own. Starting those initial sales means, a marketing budget and I know a lot of FBA sellers that spend money on Amazon ads continuously to keep their products ranked.

Even a small budget of $10 a day can be enough to start seeing significant sales for your product. It won't take long before you know exactly how much it costs per sale in marketing and can adjust your continuous marketing budget accordingly.

Graphic design and copy writing: Most of the budget items for starting an FBA business are something you probably can't do yourself. Graphic design of logos and copy writing your sales material is one place you might be able to save money with a DIY strategy.

I would still get a professional logo developed from a freelancer on Fiverr. You can try a few freelancers for $5 each and then pick the best idea. Even if you go the inexpensive route and write your own marketing material to launch your store, consider hiring someone to review it after sales start coming in.

Trademark for your brand: This is more of an optional cost to start an Amazon FBA business but totally necessary for the future. You're going to be putting thousands into developing your brand and how customers see your company, you need to protect that investment with a trademark or someone can just start their own company under the same name.

How Much Does Starting Amazon FBA Cost as a Reseller?

Startup costs for an Amazon FBA reseller business are simpler but more uncertain than the private-label business model.

With the reseller strategy, you're simply looking for things you can buy cheaply and resell at a higher price on Amazon. There are apps you can use to instantly compare prices of something on Amazon but it's still a very time-intensive business.

Inventory Costs and Shipping: This all depends on what you're buying to resell but can easily reach $1,000 to buy an initial inventory and ship to Amazon's warehouses. You want to buy in large quantities if possible. It's difficult enough finding things for sale on Amazon with enough markup over your in-person costs to make it worthwhile, you might as well buy as many as you can when you find something.

Photography and Video Costs: You usually won't need custom photography or video for the reseller business model. Check the manufacturer's website for product images or look for other Amazon pages selling the product.

Amazon Pro Account: You'll still need to open a Pro account for $40 but this is relatively minor.

Marketing Costs: Marketing costs are still a big expense in the reselling strategy. You're usually going to be competing with other FBA resellers in the same product so you'll need to rank your store with those consistent sales. A marketing budget of $500 will usually suffice here as well.

On the upside, you probably won't need to spend quite as much in on-going marketing because you'll be selling products that already have some brand recognition. Customers will be more familiar with the product versus your private-label business and won't need quite as much convincing to buy.

You won't need to register your items or get UPC codes because they will already have these from the original seller. You can seemingly also just reuse and rewrite a lot of the advertising copy from the original seller's website or find pages of the product already for sale on Amazon.

You can truly start an Amazon FBA reseller business for less than $1,000 if you're buying less expensive products. The reseller strategy is simpler than creating your own branded products but it's more time-intensive in the long run and I believe more limited on profit.

CHAPTER 14

TIME TO THINK BIGGER? SCALING YOUR AMAZON BUSINESS

I'd all like to create the kind of business which grows sustainably, provides us with a solid income and gives us the freedom to make the lifestyle choices I'd wish to have. There are many stories circulating of sellers who are unquestionably killing it through FBA and jetting their debt-free selves wherever they please.

What is the difference from these highly successful sellers and the rest? What factors provide an edge when it comes to climbing your business? Here's what I've found:

Stay above Your Numbers

Successful sellers sell huge volumes and make a profit from them; wildly successful sellers are those who stay firmly on top of the vital numbers of their business.

This includes having a good grasp of exactly what they are making on every product they sell. Many people focus too much attention on metrics which are really only vanity. This means that they are only paying close attention to measures which may make them look good on the surface, but become meaningless when you dig down to the truth.

For example, there are sellers who will gaze starry-eyed at their gross revenue; "I sold $500,000 worth of products!" Pure vanity. It's quite possible to sell $500,000 worth of products but be operating at a loss. Obviously in this case, you should be more concerned with net profit.

Margin is another one to be careful of. Have you got the right measures in place? This means you should be focusing on your adjusted gross margin — the amount that is left over once you take out all overhead costs.

On average, FBA seller's usually make 15% – 20% adjusted gross margin, but the high volumes of sales which are made possible by the Amazon platform help to keep their businesses doing well. If any of your products are making less than this, you're giving yourself very little room to move, especially if you want to stay competitively priced. If that's the case, you may want to investigate either raising your prices or moving on to a different product — one which you can make a reasonable margin.

Inventory Management

If you want to be able to scale your Amazon business, you need to have a good grasp of inventory management for each product you have. Are you losing valuable sales to stock-outs? Do you have inventory languishing in the warehouse, costing you storage fees and effectively tying up your cash on the shelf?

The bigger you grow, the more products you have to manage, so knowing these details can become more difficult. This is where having good inventory management software for FBA (such as forecastly), can help you to grow your business.

Do Something You Enjoy

This is just from the point of view of your own motivation to grow a business. Some people are motivated by the idea of making money, but for most this is not a strong enough factor to keep them going when it comes to putting in the hard yards for a business.

Selling products, you are actually interested in is a great start if you want the motivation to continue, as is selling something where you have good connections who can help to promote or grow your business in some way.

Improve Your Best Seller Ranking

The best way to improve your best seller rank is simply by outselling your competition, though of course this is easier said than done. There are several factors which go into how you are positioned on Amazon and whether or not customers are enticed to buy from you. We've written about a few of them previously. You could:

- Look for ways to boost your hourly sales.
- Incorporate the right keywords into your product listings.
- Encourage more reviews of your products on Amazon.
- Spice up your product listings with better descriptions and enticing product photography.

If you're trying everything to improve sales but you're not getting the growth in your category that you'd like, you may need to look at a less competitive category or for some other factor which will give you a competitive advantage.

Have Good Systems in Place

One of the keys to scaling any business is the systems and processes you put in place. Most FBA sellers don't want to have to hire on a lot of employees, for example, that's usually a reason why they opted for FBA. No matter how big you grow, Amazon can handle your fulfillment.

So, if you don't want an entire team of staff (or, if you want to make it easier to hire on one or two people and quickly get them up to speed), having simple, scalable systems is the way to go. This includes having the right tools to automate your processes as much as you can.

18 BIG MISTAKES NEW AMAZON SELLERS CAN'T AFFORD TO MAKE

Notwithstanding if you're selling on Amazon as a beginner, there are some mistakes you could easily make without realizing it. There's a lot of small print in those requirements, and Amazon put them in place for a reason – everything they create is driven by the shopper experience.

Having said that, below are some of the leading avoidable mistakes Amazon sellers make when setting up accounts, selling on Amazon, and managing Amazon orders.

Amazon Account Setup Fails

The Amazon Seller Account is the place where Amazon sellers spend much of their time (varies based on agency or management automation).

This is the place where Amazon sellers have a holistic view for ongoing orders, items purchased, and what is getting listed on Amazon. This is also the place where sellers manage inventory, product performance, and define campaign settings.

Be sure you set up a solid foundation for your account and products by avoiding easy blunders.

1. Registering for More Than One Seller Account

One seller account per Amazon seller- it's that simple. And it happens to be an Amazon policy violation to have two accounts. Don't get greedy.

2. Pointing Amazon Shoppers to Your Website

Several sellers have tried including a URL in their product or seller information (such as their product inventory file or business name. This is an Amazon policy violation.

Amazon is a closed ecosystem, which can be a disadvantage for retargeting (remarketing) and branding opportunities. Amazon's marketplace design and notoriety grant your store to a large shopper base- but that comes at the price of losing the ability to point shoppers back to a seller website.

Take advantage of other selling channels and strategies to increase site traffic and retarget customer's rather than trying to game Amazon.

3. Copying Another Seller's Setup

Remember selling on Amazon is difficult, and your competitor's may be violating Amazon policy and or may not have an optimized account. Constantly review Amazon best practices, audit, test, and refine your seller account.

4. Choosing the Wrong Seller Account Type

Be sure to research and choose the type of seller account that's best for your online store.

5. Misunderstanding How Amazon Works

Don't treat Amazon like eBay or Google. Amazon operates on a fundamentally different structure than either of those shopping sites. Be sure your store is capable of handling selling on Amazon, and that your strategy is aligned with Amazon policies- so you get the highest ROI on the Amazon Marketplace.

It's also very important to calculate your Amazon spend, and forecast profit margins before you go full throttle on Amazon.

6. Including Sales or Coupons in Your Product Title

It can be exceedingly tempting to include a coupon, sale or store marketing message in your product title to make your store stand out on Amazon. However, this is a clear

Amazon policy violation, and Amazon will hurt you more in the long run than any short-term benefits.

Avoid any title information with: "20% off", "Lowest Price", your URL or other information that may be construed as promotional. Amazon will eschew any product information which isn't descriptive of the product itself.

7. Using Non-Amazon Sanctioned Categories

Amazon stresses that product categories match Amazon's (Amazon.com) browse tree. Review Amazon's inventory file templates for correct product information formatting, including product title information. (Templates vary based on seller inventory)

8. Including Information in Your Product Titles Amazon Doesn't Allow

Amazon titles should follow Amazon's policies to the T. Product titles should be 100 characters (max), start with the product brand if possible, and include numerals.

9. Adding Promotional Text in Images

If you haven't caught on Amazon doesn't much care for any of your trading promotional material- anywhere near its marketplace. Avoid   any messaging or product

120

information which Amazon might view as a violation. Avoid any messaging which includes "Sale", "Free Shipping", or a similar promotional feel.

Realistically, including that type of information in an image is a bit distorted anyway.

10. Using Main Images Featuring Colored Backgrounds or Lifestyle images.

Common pictures best practices advocate using a white background. Amazon's image policy for the main image follows this guideline. On look at some of the product pictures on eBay and you can understand how this policy benefits your bottom line and Amazon clients.

11. Incorporating Image Borders, Watermarks, Text or Other Descriptions

Amazon image policy is strict. Amazon isn't playing around with its user experience, which is impacted heavily by product images.

12. Expensive Shipping

Nothing sends an online shopper running faster than over-priced shipping. Remember your Buy Box share and

Amazon selling status rely (in part) on your reviews- those for your online store and your products. Bad or expensive shipping policies may mean more immediate profits, but will negatively impact your Amazon selling success.

13. Late Shipping

Amazon customers generally note that they appreciate the ease of shopping on Amazon, but prize Amazon's cheap, and fast shipping policies. Your competitors (and Amazon) will feature fast and reliable shipping speed. Be honest with your shipping dates, and realistically consider what speed and shipping price your store can manage.

14. Sneaking in Marketing Collateral with Packing Materials

Usually, I recommend using Fulfillment by Amazon (depending on your store, fulfillment needs, and budget) to benefit from Amazon's shipping speed and customer service. In which case there's very small chance that anything promotional will get by Amazon. Nevertheless, if you're handing your own fulfillment, anything featuring your store may likely confuse or worse disappoint Amazon shoppers.

Review Amazon's Seller Shipping Rates, Fulfillment by Amazon (FBA) and fulfillment policies before choosing a fulfillment method. Remember to consider the cost of shipping to Amazon, returns, and related fulfillment variables.

15. Managing Your Account Based on Email Notifications

If you're using email to make Amazon changes, you're not managing your Amazon account effectively. Remember emails can get lost, deleted, or missed easily.

Proactively respond to customer needs, manage inventory and handle account activity. If you're in over your head, consider leveraging agency resources or outsourcing data management.

16. Paying for Positive Feedback

Amazon relies heavily on user trust—a metric they value dearly:

"Customer satisfaction is one of the most important performance measures we use to determine how well you are doing as a seller on Amazon. The Customer Metrics page provides reports that give you greater insight into how you are doing with respect to customer satisfaction."-Amazon

It's vital that you monitor and improve the variables which influence your customer metrics score, including shopper reviews for your store. However, gaming the system isn't going to push the needle in your favor enough to warrant the risk.

17. Getting Upset with Customers

Sometimes Amazon customers are unreasonably demanding or argumentative. You're guaranteed to encounter an overly-needy or irate person more than once when selling on Amazon. Avoid arguing with these shoppers at all costs.

18. Thinking Amazon Shoppers Read

Your Amazon clients aren't thoroughly reading (if at all) your policies. Even more likely, many people who have bought your items haven't read the product description entirely.

State your policies clearly, and in multiple places. Kindly reiterate policies in customer interactions, but don't forget its unlikely shoppers have read your store policy or the product description for what they've purchased.

CHAPTER 15

USING AMAZON FBA FOR EBAY
FULFILLMENT

Did you know that Amazon FBA can be used to fulfill orders across several channels? Using Amazon's state of the art fulfillment network could be just what you may need to provide faster shipping for you.

Did you know that Fulfillment by Amazon (FBA) isn't just for Amazon traders? If you sell on eBay or your own web store, you can also benefit of Amazon's fulfillment network.

Using FBA could allow your selling to grow by giving you access to immense logistical expertise, but it does come at a price. Amazon charges premium rates for FBA and, if you don't pay attention it can be expensive especially if stock doesn't sell.

Order fulfillment is a major headache for multi-channel sellers. Getting it right is crucial if you want to succeed. There are benefits to using FBA—but does the service and its costs suit your business?

I break down the practical implications and discuss the pros and cons of mastering eBay fulfillment by using Amazon

FBA. I'll also look at how the recently changed prices of multi-channel fulfillment will affect online sellers.

How does an eBay seller go Amazon FBA?

You'll need an Amazon Seller Central account to begin. Once you're registered and logged in, follow these steps:

- Go to Multi-Channel Fulfillment in the FBA settings.
- Submit your order fulfillment requirements with either a simple online form, upload a bulk file or integrate Amazon with your web store.
- Lastly, ship your inventory to an Amazon fulfillment center.

There are no minimum requirements and you can send as many items as you want. It is worth noting that as this is not a product sold through Amazon. Customer service will be handled by you.

Amazon decides which fulfillment center you use based on factors like size, product type and storage needs, as well as location. You can select your own courier or use Amazon's discounted service.

When your item is received, Amazon scans the FBA barcode sticker. These stickers are inexpensive and can be purchased easily. When you get an order and place it with Amazon, the company picks, packs and ships the item. You can monitor its progress using Amazon's online tracking system.

TOP 5 BENEFITS OF AMAZON FBA

1. It's giving you free time

Have you ever tried doing the order fulfillment by yourself? You have to speak to the potential buyer, pack your product and prepare the package for shipping. Then you have to physically drop it at your local post office. (And more often than not, there's a long queue there!)

2. It is a steroid for your business

This point is on e-commerce in general but it drives home a point that you can leverage FBA with.

Not only are more people putting items and buying from their e-cart, the proliferation of online shopping is still rapidly growing in USA. (This is also true world-wide and we will explore more about this soon.)

3. Tagging onto Amazon's perks!

Treat your customer's right with the added bonus of delivering your product the next day or two.

Amazon is also a household brand which your customers love and trust. There's a report that states that half of millennial today would rather give up sex and alcohol than to give up Amazon!

4. Win the Buy Box and qualify for Amazon Prime!

The Buy Box is akin to a competitive sport where various sellers selling the exact same item will compete for the coveted prize; which is winning the Buy Box.

While there are many factors that affects the chances of winning the Buy Box, one of them is using FBA.

By using FBA, the chances of you winning the Buy Box spot over other sell-fulfilled sellers are significantly higher. It has become a new norm for sellers to head to FBA just to get the Buy Box.

You will also be automatically qualified for Amazon Prime shipping – Prime members can get free 2-day shipping for your products.

These Prime members are customers ready to buy and when they see that they can get the free 2-day shipping on your product, you will be viewed as a trusted seller. This in turn helps bring in the moolah!

5. Profits Kaching!

Since Amazon have taken care of all the heavy lifting in your business for you, you can focus on areas that matters.

Think that the fees are too high? Think again.

The cost that you would have spent on setting up a large and efficient logistics machine is no small investment. On top of that, the amount of advertising you will invest is minimal as they are all congregated in a single platform which Amazon have spent years building. In short, your customers are already on Amazon.

It is an absolute privilege to be selling on Amazon as you are paying less labor and administrative cost on the warehousing, shipping and customer service.

CHAPTER 16

10 TIPS FOR SELLING ON AMAZON

1. Perfectionate Your Product

Fastly in 10 words or fewer, describe what you're selling. You need to be an absolute expert on your product or else your buyers will sniff out that you don't know what you're talking about. Take all the time is necessary to learn everything you can about your items so that when the occasion arises, you have an answer to all questions asked.

2. Register as a Professional Seller

There's a bit more involved than simply signing up with Amazon, uploading product descriptions and calling yourself a merchant. You can technically do that, yes, but it won't pay off in the long run. Not only will you save money on the commission on each item sold, but you can also upload items that aren't available anywhere else on Amazon and sell in previously restricted categories.

3. Keep Prices Flexible

There are two ways to create a cost for something: the price you want to sell it at, and the one it will sell at. Sometimes, the two intersect, but it doesn't happen very often. For the rest of the times, you should look at repricing software to compete with the best of them.

4. Sell What People Want

You may think macaroni necklaces are just the best thing in the world, but if enough people don't agree with you, then your sales will be kind of meagre, to say the least. I am not saying to completely abandon your dreams and passions, but to complement it with sure-fire money-makers. For example, sell the macaroni necklaces along with other types, diversifying and offering a decent selection of what people want.

5. Automate Your Listings

There's no doubt being an online merchant will mean a lot of tough work, but you can create several handy shortcuts for yourself that will add plenty of time back to your life. One of those is to use an API to automate your listings, letting technology do the heavy lifting for you. There are plenty of software programs out there, so it's just a matter of finding the one that works best for you.

6. Sell in the Middle Ground

If you've been reading so far, it may be tempting to think that selling the most popular items on Amazon is a surefire recipe for success. But when you think about it, how many merchants out there are selling Xbox systems and iPods? Plenty, which makes competing with them pretty tough. Instead, widen your horizon to the top 1,000 items or so, giving yourself a big middle ground to deal with but still with plenty of profit potential.

7. Optimize Product Listings

This is probably easiest if you're just starting out on Amazon, as everything is still a blank slate. If you're an established seller, it can be easy to lapse into bad habits and forget about optimizing your listings. Don't spend a day or two going over the quality of images, writing, keywords and everything else.

8. Play by the Rules

Yeah, Amazon's really big and there are going to be several cases all the time when something slips by. But if you continually skirt under the radar. It's just not worth it, as it can result in bad reviews, fewer sales and even being booted off Amazon.

MEDIA SELLING - FIVE STEPS TO RUNNING A SUCCESSFUL AMAZON BUSINESS

When starting a media trading business, just like any other kind of business, you need investment capital. Depending on how quick you want your business to take off, you will need more money. The bulk of your spending will be in the beginning, as you will need to purchase the proper equipment.

If you are not the kind of person who is willing to go 100 miles from home to get inventory, you probably will not be nearly as successful in this business as you could be.

1. Years ago, media scouts used to guess the price of the items by site, and buy what they thought they could sell for a good price. If you try that now, you will be losing out on incredible amounts of money. Now, an amazing piece of technology is used, called a scanner. By scanning the bar code of a media item, it gives you the prices of the items on Amazon almost instantly. I recommend using the $400 scanner from ASellerTool.com, as it is cheap, but efficient. This service costs $30 per month to maintain.

2. Sign up for FBA (Fulfillment By Amazon), at Amazon.com. It is $40 per month, but this service will pay itself off incredibly fast, you don't have to spend hours packing, and the shipping is fast. Buyers prefer buying something from FBA, as there is fast shipping and great customer service. With FBA, you can price your items lower than the $3.99 + 1c, allowing you to get an edge on your competition. Never sell something below $3.25.

3. FBAPower (FBAPower.com) is a service that will increase your efficiency of FBA that much you will not want to go without it. Using a $70 USB laser scanner, you can scan fast your items into the system. This lets you box up 50-70 pounds of media products taking about 40 seconds per item. In these 40 seconds, you need to examine fast the item, click its condition, and stick the special bar code sticker on it. This type of service costs $40 per month.

4. You will need a thermal printer. A printer, that prints with heat. I recommend getting a Dymo Thermal Label Printer. This will allow you to print without ink, and very quickly. These labels hold the bar codes of each item you send to the FBA warehouse. This printer costs about $100, and the rolls of labels tend to cost around $12.50 per roll. This seems to be cheap, as label rolls tend to have a lot on them.

CHAPTER 17

THE ADVANTAGES AND DISADVANTAGES OF USING FBA

You pay a small fee each month and in return, Amazon takes care of packing and shipping your orders. You send your inventory to Amazon so that every time you get a sale, they send pickers through their warehouse to select the items and send it to its new owner. If anything goes wrong with the order or delivery, Amazon takes care of all. They also offer help in the way of 24/7 customer service in the languages of the marketplaces it sells in and provide tracking information.

With that being said let's now take a look at what the advantages and disadvantages of FBA are.

Advantages of using FBA

Frees Up Time: You can't put a price tag on having time to grow your business and focus on strengthening it.

Storage Space: It's entirely taken care of, and you don't have to worry about stepping over boxes to reach your bed or kitchen.

Reputation: Amazon's got a solid name and buyers trust it. When you back up your line with Amazon, you increase your chances of landing a sale.

Shipping Protocols: Don't want to hassle yourself with complicated customs regulations and shipping practices? You don't even have to make it a whisper of a thought.

Amazon Prime: FBA translates into automatic qualification for Amazon Prime, which your Amazon Prime buyers will be very happy about.

Returns: Amazon will take care of all of that for you, from talking to the buyer to sending them a new product.

Sell Volume: The FBA fees, along with Amazon's commission, may seem like it's hard to get a profit until you see just how much more your sell rate has increased.

Listings: Yup, you can use other people's listings for your own, adding even more time saved by using FBA.

Money-making Tips: Bundle and multipack your items for even bigger profits.

DISADVANTAGES OF FBA

Cost: FBA isn't free, and can eat up your profit margin if you sell large, heavy and/or inexpensive items.

Co-mingling: Your inventory is sorted by like, and the product that goes to your buyer may not necessarily be the one you sent Amazon.

Order Volume: It can be tricky to ascertain how full you need to keep your inventory, particularly around busy times like holidays.

Control: You give up a lot of it because Amazon packs and ships their way, so you don't get to suss out cheaper materials or routes.

Sending to Amazon: You have to follow very specific ways of sending your inventory to Amazon, like labelling products individually.

Competition: I don't want to say you'll have to start sleeping with one eye open, but you should definitely be aware of Amazon cutting into your potential revenue.

Part-Time vs. Full-Time: If selling on Amazon is your sole occupation, it can pay off to use FBA. But if you're a casual seller, then the costs may cut into your profit margin too much.

Patience: It may take time to see a profit, and the trial-and-error period where you may be in the hole for a while can be uncomfortable to bear.

What to Sell? Market research is necessary to know what the efficient-selling items are and which ones to steer clear of.

CHAPTER 18

HOW TO BECOME A TOP-RATED AMAZON SELLER

From its humble roots in 1994, Amazon has grown from a small online retailer to become one of the world's largest online stores with outnumbered individuals, businesses, and companies using its platform to sell their items.

Some traders do not know the most effective and efficient ways on how to make money selling on amazon. Some of the best ways to sell your products on Amazon and become a top-rated seller have been mentioned above.

Ensure You Have Enough Products

Though it is important to have a few products when you start selling on Amazon, it is important to have enough products to cater for demand in case people like your products and you begin getting more orders. This ensures that return customers and those who have been referred do not look for alternative sellers.

Your Products Should Be Affordable with Flexible Pricing

The best way on how to make money selling on Amazon is by selling your products at affordable rates. Check your competitor's prices and adjust accordingly. Though this might not get you a huge profit margin at first, it is the best way to get and retain more customers.

In addition, you should be flexible in pricing. If you are the only seller of a given product and there is increased demand, you can slightly push the prices up to increase profitability.

Use Amazon Marketing Tools and Amazon Seller Central

Another way on how to make money selling on Amazon is by utilizing existing Amazon marketing tools including Tags, Listmania and Likes which will help your products get more visibility. Additionally, Amazon seller central provides regular reports that can help you analyze your sells, know potential customers and find out the effectiveness of your marketing and promotions.

Become an Amazon Featured Merchant

Being a featured merchant on Amazon will not only get your products noticed, but will also make you reputable and trusted among potential customers? Though Amazon does not say how sellers become featured merchant, you can easily get to that list by having good sales, little or no customer complaints and excellent customer reviews. You should also ensure that you adhere to all Amazon selling rules, regulations and policies to avoid getting banned.

Understand all expenses and fees

The most effective and efficient way on making money selling on Amazon is by understanding all associated fees and costs. If you are a seller who buys products then sells them on Amazon, your selling cost must be able to accommodate all your costs and amazon fees. Amazon charges fees for trading and referrals.

HOW DOES SMM HELP TO INCREASE YOUR AMAZON SALES?

If you are a seller on Amazon, it is e important to do right marketing for getting an increased number of sales. There are some established marketing methods, which give amazing results if applied. Due to huge competition on Amazon, every seller tries to apply peculiar strategies to get valuable customers to his/her product listing. To get a hold of this unconventional change, many sellers have followed an extraordinary way of media marketing to boost their Amazon sales.

The media marketing services are the most excellent way to generate real impact on ones' business. Due to rapid and efficient results, a number of Amazon sellers are taking help of social media marketing experts. Media marketing basically means an approach to endorse a company or business website via various social media channels such as Facebook, LinkedIn, Twitter, etc. This method of business

141

development has redefined globe of communication. Furthermore, with right social media services, you have all chances to drive a massive amount of traffic to your listing on Amazon.

Hiring an Amazon SEO Company who is well-familiar with social media marketing techniques can promote and provide all information related to their products within huge series of networking. They can help raise various ground-breaking proposals through such broad networks to reach your potential consumers in a big way.

Benefits of Media marketing

Social Networking Sites

Regular updates and information about your Amazon products can be posted on different social networking web sites. In fact, these sites are frequently visited by millions of visitors every day. You can also integrate appropriate pictures, content, coupons, and even videos for selling promotion.

Accordingly, there is no shortage of social networking websites to popularize your selling business. On the other hand, it is recommended to hire a professional marketing company for the same to handle things perfectly for your product advertising and increase your returns all together. You should make social connections and facilitate your business reach your budding customers' world-wide by hiring an Amazon SEO Company.

Blogging

A reliable Social media marketing agency takes up the assignment of creating a blog for your Amazon products and updating it frequently. Blogging can be highly informative that is utilized to drive massive traffic to your product listing. Therefore, it is extremely important to make sure if the Social media firm does this task professionally.

CHAPTER 19

MAKE MONEY SELLING USED BOOKS ON AMAZON

First of all, look for all the books around your home that you no longer need. Once you have your books ready then register on the Amazon site which will literally take ten minutes or so.

Register the books on the site is extremely easy as you enter the international book standard number and it will automatically bring up your book. You then can see the market cost applied for your used book.

I would recommend entering your book price at one penny less than the nearest person which ensures you get a low-price tag next to your book. You then just click and complete your listing. Amazon will then send you a sold dispatch now email when the book is sold and you mail the book to your customer.

Once you need more stock, I recommend looking at the local charity shops and libraries. Also, car boot sales and fairs are very good too. I have bought books for 25p and sold them for 20 pound and this happens weekly.

Not every category of book will sell extremely well so it is very important to avoid modern fiction titles. There are literally thousands of used books in this category on amazon and you will not be able to generate income with these types of books.

You should really be looking for older books with a hobby connotation. Good examples of these could be music, religion, self-help, military, arts and crafts, sports and poetry to name but a few.

It is very easy to get the hang of and in time you will easily be able to identify what sells and what does not sell. I also personally sell DVD's online too but you must make sure that your DVD works before sending out to a customer because good customer feedback is very important in this business. Having said that DVD's are fast moving items and can easily make you a lot of money.

If you have an amazon library online of about one hundred books or so then you can be expecting to sell about 30 books or so a month. When you reach this level of sales then it makes it worthwhile to become an amazon book seller. This costs 25 pound a month but also cuts the 85p charge that amazon puts on your account every time a book sell. Of course, Amazon needs to make some income from the arrangement with yourself but as you can see the 30 book per month and over limit makes it a viable business decision.

Another top tip is to try and keep your books small to medium in size to save on the postage costs. Amazon are quite generous and will give you a good postage allowance when selling your books but on very large books you will actually lose out.

Having said that school textbooks and educational books are very good sellers and can attract prices over 20 pounds or so therefore I would make an exception for those type of books.

This really is an easy business to operate and amazon provide an excellent online forum so you can talk to other amazon sellers and also gets lots of good tips and advice.

PROS AND CONS OF SELLING BOOKS ON AMAZON

Have you published yourself as an author? If so, have you already decided where are you going to trade your books? What about auction books on Amazon? The idea sounds fascinating and you know that, actually thousands of traditionally and self-published authors have adopted this platform as their main point of sale for their books.

If you have still a decision to make, you should better evaluate the pros and cons of selling books on Amazon. Here are some ideas to get you started:

Advantages

• One of the main advantages of selling books on Amazon is that it can be really profitable for you. Amazon pays for part of the shipping costs and even this may not cover for the whole expense, it will definitely increase your profits.

• Many sellers also find fascinating the fact that they can add plenty of information on their books' description that makes them peculiar to the eyes of the potential buyers and, needless to say, also increases your chances of selling them. For example, if you have an autographed book from a popular author, it will definitely be much more attractive and valuable for some of his avid readers and fans.

• Other important advantage of selling your books on Amazon is that your Amazon gives you the email and physical address of the person purchasing your books. That is very valuable data as you can create your own clients' list and keep them updated on any new titles you have for sale or any main discount or treat you have to offer them.

Disadvantages

• Your customers won't receive free super saver shipping on orders over a certain amount. This may seriously discourage some potential buyers from purchasing the books directly from you if they are also sold by Amazon directly.

It's advisable to ship your books 48 hours after receiving the purchase order. This can make selling books on Amazon quite messy if your books are popular and you receive continuous purchase requests.

THIRD-PARTY SELLERS' COVERAGE FOR AMAZON SUSPENSION

More than product returns and cart abandonment, third-party sellers on Amazon fear losing sales and access to their accounts due to suspension whether it is valid or not.

Getting banned from Amazon can ruin not only your finances but your life regardless of how long the suspension is.

That especially holds true if you use the Amazon marketplace as your main source of income; you don't have an eCommerce site, a bricks-and-mortar shop or a regular job as a backup.

When you get banned, it's like you lost a limb as you lose the ability to pay for your everyday expenses.

Various reasons can lead to a third-party seller's suspension from Amazon: late response or shipment, high order defect rate, high cancelation rate, etc.

There are also painful instances when a seller gets banned not for their own doing, but as a result of their competitor's devious stratagems.

Did you know there are sellers on Amazon who would go to the extent of paying large amounts of money in exchange for fake reviews on their biggest competition's product?

It's a good thing you can do something about that now thanks to the Amazon suspension coverage which some insurance companies offer.

Protect yourself and your business

Anyone can be banned from Amazon without notice regardless of their seller rating or performance metrics.

It is an ordeal which you never want to suffer, but the odds are high that you can avoid it, so might as well find a way to protect yourself and your business just in case it befalls you.

Lloyd's of London, which has gained global fame by ensuring famous celebrities' body parts, is one of the insurance companies that are offering insurance plans to compensate seller's for lost sales and expenses during an Amazon suspension.

Businesses of all sizes can be insured; coverage limits range from $50,000 to $1,000,000 for a period of 30 to 180 days.

Monthly premiums depend on many factors, among them are your annual sales, and how long you've been selling on Amazon and your average feedback rating.

Even sellers who have been suspended in the past can apply for coverage, but this too will influence their premiums.

Be reinstated and receive payout

In case you get banned from Amazon, you can get your account reinstated within 72 hours aside from your payout.

The amount you will receive will be based on your midpoint gross sales volume plus regular day-to-day expenses.

Note that your coverage will only be effective after the waiting period which is stipulated in your policy.

During that length of time, you are expected to push your day-to-day expenses, hence classed as your insurance deductible.

If Amazon raises your suspension before that period is over, you won't be able to collect money from your policy.

Getting suspended from Amazon is no joke, so it's good to know that third-party sellers now have an option to preserve what they've strived so hard for.

CHAPTER 20

DON'T GET BANNED FROM SELLING ON
AMAZON - IT COULD BE FOREVER

Amazon.com offers small businesses and entrepreneurs' ready access to a huge customer market for their products. Of course, sellers pay a price for the chance to trade on Amazon's good name, internet saturation and global market reach. Not only do private sellers often find themselves in direct competition with the internet colossus for products and services, but Amazon holds all the cards. To protect its own reputation and maintain a satisfied customer base, Amazon's sellers' agreement and many rules stack the deck firmly in Amazon's favor.

In order to sell on Amazon.com, sellers must follow an exacting list of expectations that dictate how and when they interact with their customers at every point in the sales process. Fail to meet Amazon's performance expectations and you could receive a not particularly cheerful "Hello from Amazon.com" letter notifying you that your account has been blocked and your sales listings terminated. And, by the way, Amazon will be hanging onto your money for the next 90 days to cover any unresolved financial issues.

For businesses that rely on Amazon.com as a primary conduit to customers and order fulfillment, receiving one of Amazon's computer-generated "Hello" letters can spell disaster. A big part of the problem is that the letters are computer-generated. Computer algorithms don't care if you didn't respond to a customer within the required 24 hours because you were hospitalized or on vacation. They're completely unsympathetic that your approval rating appears to be in the toilet not because you provide poor service but because the only customers who have bothered to offer feedback are dissatisfied ones.

Many Amazon.com sellers complain that they've been unfairly booted off Amazon because they've fallen victim to the "law of negative averages" in which a small number of negative comments can, if they outnumber positive feedback, result in a negative feedback score. For example, if out of 50 sales, 47 customers are satisfied, but only 1 post positive feedback while 2 dissatisfied customers post negative comments, Amazon's trackers will record a negative average and you'll soon be the recipient of a letter from alliance @ amazon.com, Amazon's enforcement department.

What sends sellers into a panic is the phrase "the closure of an account is a permanent action," implying that you will be forever banned from selling on Amazon. And the ban will not only affect you, but anyone Amazon's online trackers can connect to your name, street address or email address. All is not lost; however, sellers can petition Amazon for reinstatement and a number have done so successfully. The process is not easy; and, if reinstated, you can expect Amazon to scrutinize your account carefully for some time (and hang onto your money while they do so); but you can get back in the game.

1. Look carefully at the points made in the letter you receive from alliance @ amazon.com. Review your consumer metrics to see if you're falling short of expectations.

2. Respond promptly via email, explain that you feel your suspension is unfair and rebut each charge with as much factual information as possible. Attach pertinent records or letters from consumers and offer your explanation of any negative feedback.

3. If you've failed to meet Amazon's performance targets, review your sales practices and provide an action plan to correct the problem.

4. Plead your case, emphasizing your sales and customer service record and pointing out how your product benefits consumers.

5. Monitor your email for Amazon's decision.

To prevent being terminated, keep a close eye on your email and regularly review Amazon's agreements and help pages as Amazon may change its procedures and guidelines at any time without notifying sellers. Monitor the customer metrics Amazon provides and compare your performance to the Amazon's seller performance targets to make certain you are hitting the expected benchmarks.

What Is Amazon's Choice?

So, you've received an email that one of your products have received an Amazon's Choice badge. What is it? How can it help your business?

WHAT IS AMAZON'S CHOICE?

Amazon's Choice is a feature that helps people save time and effort when looking for common, everyday items. Initially meant for Alexa-enabled devices like the Amazon Echo and the Echo dot, this feature has now paved its way to the website and the Amazon app.

The Amazon's Choice badge is a recognition given to select products that meet a certain criteria. The criteria are a closely guarded secret; however, judging from products that received the badge - highly rated products and well-priced ones with Prime Shipping are the ones usually selected.

Amazon's Choice vs Best Sellers

Amazon's Choice is mainly a suggestion for customers buying a product for a specific query for the first time. So, if you have looked for pet seat cover for the first time, this would be on top of the list. When you asked Alexa for a car seat cover for the first time, Alexa will suggest products with the badge first.

Best Sellers on the other hand, are rated by the volume of sales of the product (while taking into account the historical data), relative to other products in the category. The rank is based on sales, not reviews nor ratings. So, unlike Amazon's Choice you may find that some Best Sellers have low review ratings.

How to Get the Amazon's Choice Badge?

To receive such recognition, the seller must have an Amazon Prime, has received positive ratings from the clients and provide excellent service (mainly focused on fast delivery). These factors may or may not be the reason products get picked as we know that the reason a product is chosen is a closely guarded secret, but nothing changes if you try to improve on these criteria.

The badge cannot be bought like an advertisement would nor can it be suggested. There isn't any means to suggest your product to Amazon for suitability.

CHAPTER 21

WHAT ENCOURAGES PEOPLE TO BUY ON AMAZON?

Every seller who is having problems on Amazon wants to know the answer to this question. After all, if you make out how to stimulate people to buy your products on Amazon, then you should have no trouble boosting your sales, which is the leading goal. The golden rule is to offer people what they need, because that is what they will pay out for.

In case, if you have a product or service to sell, you are advised to present it to your potential customers as something they wish for. You should spotlight on the benefits of your products and make them feel like it is something they without doubt should have. Make them think like they can't live without your product.

Most individuals make a purchase on Amazon, because they get happiness from their purchase. Amazon platform offers the most convenient and easier online shopping experience in comparison to other e-commerce sites. While it is the most important factor, many other triggers can motivate them to whisk out their wallets. For example, if you can connect your product to consumers in a way that can facilitate them save more time, have comfortable experience, and increases their enjoyment.

As a seller on Amazon, you should take advantage of the opportunities that will benefit them in an optimistic way. Only then you can encourage them to take suitable action. Once you realize what they would like, present your product or service in such a manner that makes them consider like they can't live without it. Consequently, you should have no problem in boosting your sales on Amazon.

VIRTUAL ASSISTANTS SHARE 6 BEST TIPS ABOUT AMAZON SELLING TACTICS

Amazon is a very large online platform, to do your business. To become successful, follow some tactics of selling in Amazon and make excellent profits. Virtual Office Assistants share few selling tactics that are easy to use and highly effective. These tactics will quickly increase your sales volume and profit, without increasing your expenses.

Sell your product in Bulk:

Increase your sales by combining 2 or more related products into a special combination package. Price them with a cost that should be low when compared to the cost of buying them separately. Promote it as a special offer. Another tip you can add with this is selling them for relatively low value with the warning comment that such an offer will never happen again. For example, you're selling a product for $50, normally. Create a onetime offer that will cut the price in half and offer this for certain period.

This would create a sense of panic on anyone who would get to know about your offer. The result would be a huge rush to purchase your item! At times this would initiate a fire sale.

Listing should be simple and informative:

Include your listing description in such a way that it should be simple and informative. Avoiding using exaggerated phrases during listing; this would make your prospective customers not to believe, even if it is true. One tip you can include, while listing is to state the numbers with fractions or decimals than converting to whole number.

Emphasis your product's price in a positive way:

Make sure that the cost you include for your product or service should not distract your customers though it is comparatively high. For example, "600 Rs per year" frightens many customers away. Instead present it as "Enjoy all of this for less than 50 Rs a Month" which attracts them to the low cost.

Use a Simple Buying Procedure:

Increase your sales by making your products or services to be easily available to your customers. It is because the method of ordering should be easy and convenient for everyone to buy. Potential customers will always like to buy your products only if the method of ordering is easy and suitable for them.

Make simple buying procedures and also ensure that you have more methods of buying. Offering choices of

HOW to buy increases your sales. Use simple order form instead of shopping carts when customers come for few items.

Expose yourself in the public:

Potential customer's like to buy a product or service from familiar and trustworthy sellers. Expose yourself in such a way let your prospective customers reach you.

Publicize your real name and personal contact information. Include your name, address and phone number and professional pictures on everything you use to promote business, like including it in your web pages and email messages. Also make sure that you are there to solve their problems whenever they face with your products or services.

Reply customer enquiries promptly:

Replying to customer's inquiries and questions will surely expand your sales. If you think it's vague to answer a lot of questions, then post the answers to your most FAq on a questions and Answers page at your web site. This would help in establish healthy relationship between you and customers, which in turn leads to profitable business.

CHAPTER 22

TOP 3 SECRETS TO CONVERT YOUR NEW CUSTOMERS TO REPEAT CUSTOMERS ON AMAZON

Amazon is one of the largest online platforms. To lead an endless successful business, you as a business maker should make your existing customers happy, so they become loyal repeat clients.

Here are some few strategies that our Professional Virtual Experts shares to make of your new customers a repeat customers on Amazon.

1. Follow up your client with more offers:

This is one of the best strategies of retaining the existing customers. Clients are very interested to more offers immediately after they buy from you. Offer them another item or service related to the one they just bought. Many will accept your offer, producing a smooth sale for you. If you don't already have additional products or services, try to find or create something for them.

By offering them additional offers thereby motivating them to become repeat customers, you are one step forward in becoming a successful and smart seller.

2. Encourage your customers with prompt replies:

Make sure that you reply to your customer's queries and issues quickly. Ensure them that you are there to solve their issues at any point of time. This will build a healthy relationship between you and your prospective customers.

For repeated multiple questions use FAq in your website. This will build confidence in your products and services there by increasing your sales.

3. Welcome issues from discontented customers:

Do remember that customers are the backbone of your business. Whenever they come for your products or services ask them to give a feedback on the same, so that it may focus you as a trustworthy seller in the public. Obviously, this would gradually increase your sales.

Pay more attention on unhappy customers. Resolving their issues helps you to find a solution to a problem to improve your business. Just think how great it would be for businesses if you take care of your customers. This will make your prospective customers to advertise for you through word-of-mouth advertising which would precisely increase your sales.

6 TACTICS ON DISCOVERING THE AMAZON WEB SITE FOR YOUR WEB BUSINESS EXPANSION

The official website of Amazon.com, Inc. Became operational i.e. went online in 1995. In just under twenty years the site has become the biggest online dealer and retailer of almost every type of product or service and covers almost all categories you can think of. Whatever item you name it, they have it including products and services. This is not limited to consumer electronics, retail items, digital applications and contents, customized and branded labels, cloud computing, content production, donations and charities. Mind that Amazon started online retailing with books.

If you're thinking of launching your own start-up or want to take your existing business to the next level by going online, then Amazon's own success story will really work as a morale booster. It was once an innocuous start-up and now it is providing a platform to countless others to get started up. You too can join the bandwagon of those who have already used the amazon platform for promoting their business online and countless others who are registered online members of the Amazon online club. Take stock of the following six strategies on how best you can exploit the portal of Amazon for your business gains: -

1. Promote your products or services on Amazon.com: - Although Amazon is the largest online stocker of all sorts of products and services; it will stand you in good stead if you start with just a single product or service hitching on their 'sell on Amazon' plan. Thereafter, you can graduate to becoming a small merchant seller selling more than 10 items. You will be required to pay either a proportion or a flat amount per sale apart from a fixed fee every month. In return you'll get the benefit of using administrative, creative and technical tools to help increase your revenues.

2. Use the Amazon platform as an advertisement platform: - You can use the site for listing images of your product with lucid product details and' how to instructions. This mode of promotion is much cheaper than using the 'selling on Amazon' program as you pay on pay-per-click (PPC) basis. Using the advertisement programs also involving furnishing minimum of details as far as your product or service is concerned. You at least don't have to keep uploading price lists, inventory lists and other details.

3. You can make your online store a sort of store within a large store: - Amazon offers you the opportunity of

opening a 'webstore' if you are a greenhorn and hence inexperienced in online marketing. It's your own virtual store.

4. Use the fulfillment policy of Amazon to the hilt: -The best thing about promoting and selling through Amazon is that they undertake full responsibility of delivering your products safely to your customers, dealing with returns, and providing customer support.

5. Capitalize from Amazon's data storage and cloud computing services: - Apart from using Amazon's portal as an advertisement and selling platform you can make good use of web facilities for storing your files or valuable business data.

6. Use checkout by Amazon: - Irrespective of the online platform you're using to promote your products or services, you can always proffer 'checkout by Amazon' as a payment alternative to your customers.

CHAPTER 23

IS AMAZON KILLING SMALL ONLINE BUSINESSES?

Most people think of Amazon as an online bookstore, which manages to be both true and incredibly incorrect at the same time. Amazon started life as a bookstore, of course, one that could potentially sell you any book ever printed, but they've grown business even bigger than that.

They are an incredibly powerful retailer with a highly refined sales funnel, and it might seem impossible for a small online commerce to compete with that level of name recognition and money.

The sad truth is that for too many online businesses, Amazon will eventually kill them, if it hasn't already. Small independent book sellers, for example were some of the first retailers to embrace going online. It was hard to find out of print and rare books, so there was a prepared group of bibliophiles ready and waiting, and for a couple of years the online booksellers did well.

Until Amazon steam rollered over the top of them, using its massive economy of scale to offer both a bigger selection and better prices. There are still online booksellers out there, but the vast majority succumbed to the Amazon huge force.

Something similar has happened to online music stores and online DVD retailers as Amazon has continued to expand the range of products they offer.

But in spite of that, there are more small online businesses than ever before. The world of online commerce is more refined and more vibrant than ever before, even with some powerhouse sites taking a huge chunk of the market share.

So how do you save your online business from becoming a victim of Amazon's seemingly unstoppable growth? There are two ways that you can carve out your own unique spot on the Internet; you can do it through having a laser focus on a very specific niche, or you can do it through personality. Or you can combine the best of both worlds and use both.

Amazon does many things well, but it is still fundamentally a giant corporation, and that means it can't even begin to have the same kind of one on one interaction that a small online business can have. If you make friends with your customers, they will stick with you and even pay a premium to do business with you. Personality is something that no corporation can beat you at.

FINDING AMAZON KINDLE ACCESSORIES THAT PROTECT YOUR KINDLE

When you get an Amazon Kindle, you will want to purchase accessories with it and if you know someone who owns an Amazon Kindle an accessory would be a great gift. There are a lot of different ways to customize it. Customizing a Kindle adds personality, color, and also protect it. The most common accessories are surely chargers, covers, and reading lights. The Amazon Kindle accessories come in all colors, shapes, and sizes and prices.

Finding the perfect Kindle cover for a particular person can seem easy but very easily becomes a meticulous task, contrary to what you might have first believed. The Amazon Kindle has become very popular amongst book lovers. When looking for the best Amazon Kindle cover for yourself or someone else you should look at how well it protects the device, your preference, and personality.

Accessories are available from various online sellers on the internet. When choosing the best skin for yourself or someone else you should check the reviews and ratings for durability and quality of the particular product that you are looking at. Since cases and covers are protecting it the durability is key to a good cover, and the quality plays into saving your Amazon kindle if it is dropped. There are various kindle covers flooding the market giving you sophisticated, elegant, dark colored, pink colored and leather look. You can also find added protection for the Kindle with a magnetic snap closure to protect the front and back of the kindle. The covers also are designed to give you access to the different ports and switches on the device.

TIPS TO PROFITABLY SELL USED MEDIA ON AMAZON

When most people believe of selling online many times they automatically think EBAY While eBay remains the largest online auction marketplace their main competitor which is Amazon is also an excellent place to sell merchandise of any kind This is especially if you are selling any kind of used media such as books, music and movies, DVD, vcr. Here are some important things you need to know to successfully make a money selling on amazon.

1. Since people who buy from amazon are generally looking for the best deal it is important to be able to compete to offer the lowest price or at least be very near

the bottom. That means you will need to acquire items very cheaply.

2. The best places to find used media for very low prices that you can sell on amazon are thrift shops and garage sales.

3. If you are scouting for books you will need to be picky on what you purchase. The kind of books that do well on amazon are specific topical. Examples of good topics that do well are business and finance.

4. If you are scouting for music to sell your best bet is to stick to greatest hits or compilations.

5. Another area that is important to cut costs in is with your shipping supplies. Since your profit margin on the actual product sometimes is low you can make up for that by earning a profit on shipping. Amazon compensates you with a shipping credit. If you purchase your mailing and printing supplies at a discount wholesale store you should be able to make a profit spread between your shipping credit and your expenses.

6. If you sell more than 40 products a month upgrade to pro merchant. There is an additional 1-dollar fee on each

product you sell that every pro merchant doesn't get charged so it saves a lot of cash for high volume sellers.

C0NCLUSION

HOW TO SHIP PRODUCTS TO AMAZONS

So, you've tracked your products, contacted suppliers and received samples you're happy with, and you're now ready to start trading them to your potential clients. Since this is your first time with Amazon FBA, you're all excited and electrified until you realize and asked yourself, how will you actually supposed to do it.

How exactly do you ship your items to Amazon in the first place? What are the steps involved in getting this step done?

Before we jump to the steps, its essential to note there are two ways to do this. You can either ship the product straight from China to Amazon or ship the product to yourself or to a US-based intermediate (presuming you're selling to the US), then send it to Amazon's warehouses.

The difference lies in communication and familiarity with Amazon's requirements. If you're shipping from China, you need to instruct your suppliers to prepare the product according to Amazon specifications. You see, Amazon can reject your package if it doesn't comply with their standards. Though suppliers are usually familiar with the process, there's always the chance of miscommunication or incorrect labelling.

Sending the goods to yourself or to a US-based middleman may put you in a safer position because there's likely clearer communication, knowledge of the process, and a quality inspection before they are sent to Amazon.

Now that we've got that out of the way, below are the steps you need to take to ship your product to Amazon:

1. Prepare your shipping plan

The first step is to get all the details ready for the incoming inventory order you will be raising in Seller Central. You'll need the following information to build an incoming inventory order:

Number of Units and Cases – There are two things you need to remember. First, Amazon has a limit of 150 units per case and that boxes over 50lbs need to be marked "team lift." As long as you follow these conditions, your shipment should be okay.

Universal Product Code (UPC) – new products require a UPC which you can buy and send to Amazon as a way of telling them that you'd be introducing new products to the market.

Who does the packing and preparation? – For this part, it will be better to have your supplier's handle the preparation. With Amazon's popularity, it's rare for these suppliers not to know the processes and guidelines for shipping products to Amazon FBA.

The only thing you have to make sure is that suppliers understand Amazon's fulfilment center guidelines specific to the goods you are sending (loose products, products with expiration, etc.)

Are you going to use Amazon's FBA Label service? – Each product you ship to Amazon requires a scannable barcode for storage and fulfilment purposes.

Who's your shipping partner? – You have 2 options to choose from if you are to use a local shipping partner. You either use one of Amazon's partner carriers who will provide you the tracking numbers and barcodes (UPS recommended), or any other carrier. Just take note of the tracking number and give them to Amazon.

Weight and Size of order – You'll need to provide Amazon with details about the weight and dimension of the product you're sending. Just make sure to specify weight in pounds and dimension in inches. If your supplier will be the one sending the goods, you have to get this information from them.

Location you are shipping your products from – For the last part, you just need to give the location where the shipment will be coming from along with the tracking number associated with it.

With a couple of fulfilment centers in each marketplace, it is worth noting that Amazon may require you to divide your products into a couple of shipments so they can send them to different warehouses. The reason is simply because the delivery will be much faster if the product is spread across different locations.

Inventory placement Service

Remember what we said earlier about how Amazon distributes your items across multiple locations? Well, you can now send all of them to just one fulfilment center (though you don't get to pick the one you want) via Amazon's new service called the Inventory Placement Service.

This option isn't really something I would advise for first timers but certainly it does offer some advantages. One of these actual advantages is that you'll be doing your customers a favor, especially those who order in bulk because they'd be receiving your items in one shipment instead of separate ones.

This will also help reduce the likelihood of errors like putting on the wrong shipping labels or sending to the wrong fulfilment centers in the case of sending your inventory to many fulfilment centers.

It's also worth knowing that the feature will cost you $0.30 for each standard size unit and $1.30 for each oversized unit.

Make use of Freight Forwarders

While Amazon allows the sending of inventory from an International Supplier directly to their fulfilment centers, it's important to know that they won't take any responsibility for the shipment should something unexpected happens therefore you need to talk to your suppliers to make sure that everything goes smoothly.

Your best option is to use a freight forwarding company for the reason that, apart from taking care of your shipments and sending them to Amazon, they will also take responsibility of the customs issues and be your onsite quality assurance checker, making sure that everything's in place on your behalf.